Never Say Neigh

.

Never Say Neigh

An Adventure in Fun,

Funny, and the Power of Yes

ΩV Noah Vail
™ with Mary I. Farr

Second Edition

Published 2015 by HumorOutcasts Press
Printed in the United States of America

ISBN: 0-692-37539-2
EAN-13: 978-069237539-6

Author's website: www.noahvailpublishing.com

Illustrations by Mary I. Farr

Cover Design by Alan Pranke
Marna Poole, Editor

Printed in the United States of America

For our friend Mike Veeck,

author and champion of *Fun Is Good*

True though Slightly Embellished Contents

Introduction

Welcome to Noah's room. Some might call it a stall, as it serves as home sweet home to a horse named Noah. He's the handsome bay gelding who created this book from equal parts of fun and funny.

"Noah's room" refers to his office, his dining room, and his man cave that hosts countless games of gin rummy and cribbage. This Noah operates in a world of horse hilarity. He blogs. He travels. He philosophizes, more or less. He falls in love. He dishes on the economy as well as the human and equine condition. He also promotes important matters, such as friendship, fairness, and compassion. Noah's a good-news sort of guy who operates on the 100-watt side of life. He even earned the title of chief experience officer at Evergreen Farm. Noah's room is a perfect place for anyone who yearns for a brighter light cast upon the day. It's also a grand place to begin a yearlong adventure with him, an adventure laced with laughter, though punctuated with more than a few thought-provoking ideas.

I'm Noah's partner—he calls me Madam, or the management, depending on the current state of affairs—and I serve as his personal assistant. Some suggest I serve as his personal chef, as well as driver, housekeeper, and financial manager. Though he constantly chases new career opportunities as well as a few girlfriends, Noah mostly loves to observe others and write about them. Actually, he talks; Madam writes. Even a clever horse needs help with fan mail and Facebook pages that call for fingers. I invite you to step into Noah's room. Join him in his Comfy Sundowner horse trailer. Meet his unusual assortment of card-playing friends and of course, get acquainted with his staff of one—Madam.

Why Read This Book?

We live in difficult times with no shortage of bad news and uninvited events. Yet even difficult times cannot take away our capacity to hope—to listen, learn, laugh, and be transformed. This kind of hope enables us to grow together with others, in spite of fears and uncertainty. It opens the doors to living more fully, not as naïve sheep who turn our backs on the world and its problems but as expectant travelers, anticipating future good. One thing is clear: we gain nothing by pulling down the blinds or giving way to cynicism and despair.

Noah and his friends offer a tiny respite from stress and unease. His mission in life is to provide a refuge of merry horse-and-human encounters and creative ways to view life from the barn—or from the road, for that matter. Noah and Madam believe life deserves to be lived fully and well. They enjoy their little space on this fragile earth. They also trust that each day improves with a measure of fun and a good game of gin rummy. Most important, Noah and Madam hope their modest attempts to light up their reader's day inspire fans to leap to their feet and shout *Yes!* Yes, after all, is good for friendships. Yes broadens the possibilities for fun. Yes opens the door to new adventures, and yes can even spark up a dull workday (or, in Noah's case, a dull training program).

.

1

Who Me, an Author?

This writing life began to take shape when I moved into my new room at Evergreen Farm. Well, let me restate that: it actually became a serious enterprise due to a radio, a black plastic squawker that sits on a shelf outside my room. Now, don't get me wrong. I enjoy the smooth sounds of a little Norah Jones. I'm even a big country music fan, though all those ruined romances can get a little old. But this daily flood of irate talk radio is not my cup of tea. Shrill voices filling the airways with reckless claims make me sweat. One minute, it's a new research study warning folks to wear helmets to bed in case they fall out in the middle of an exciting dream. Next, it's grim counsel about contaminated artichokes and bogus vitamins. Or what about local coyotes snatching family pets from the backyard? And those alarming topics don't even account for the somber economic news, the housing crisis, lost jobs, and all measure of thorny health care problems. While I don't mean to speak lightly about serious issues, I'm pretty sure my migraine headaches have something to do with the constant stream of cheerless news.

One would think the landlord in this place could change the station to a St. Paul Saints baseball game. But no, someone apparently enjoys a daily dose of despair. Maybe this radio thing paralyzes humans or causes them to stare blankly into space. In any case, the radio has been casting a chilly shadow over my delightful new room.

Most of my new stable mates ignore the radio, but I've noticed Madam often stops to take in a bit of talk-show twaddle. Then, instead of handing over a carrot or changing the station to quiet jazz, she sighs deeply. Next, she gives a recurring speech about how *we* might have to go live with her daughter in Vermont or become wards of the state if economic matters don't improve. I have to wonder about this *we* business, as I'm clearly too big to live in a one-room apartment in Manchester, Vermont. I also don't know of any state that takes in horses, even in a pinch.

Maybe she's thinking of the University of Minnesota's veterinary school. In that case, who knows what it could mean for the two of us? I happen to know a draft horse named Ned who enjoys a career as a blood donor at the U's large animal clinic. They feed him well, and he enjoys his Shetland pony companion, but it would take more than a bag of Equine Senior and a horse house pet to lure me into that profession.

I suppose I could consider law enforcement. Then I imagine, for a moment, trying to round up a troop of unruly Vikings football fans loping down the Nicollet Mall. If this confounded talk radio is speaking truth about dismal job prospects, things look mighty grim for me.

Something else is weighing on my mind these days. Shortly after I arrived in Minnesota, Madam accepted a work assignment that requires her to travel. So now, when we are just getting acquainted, I don't get to see her on a daily basis. Plus, she insists on packing up her elderly Jack Russell terrier and the fluff-muffin cat to keep her company on the road. The three of them drive off like a scene out of *Sanford and Son*. Away they go, motoring down Interstate 94, transporting everything but the family ironing board—I mean, a kitty litter box, a dog kennel, coolers, suitcases, and computers. And let me not forget the hairball pets, with their little round backsides parked smack in the passenger seat. By the way, the cat has assumed ownership of the car. No kennel for him. He prefers to parade around loose, occasionally perching atop a suitcase, waving at passing drivers. And he's not shy about using his kitty box, while nearly asphyxiating the other passengers in the process. Both the dog and cat treat this unfortunate employment development as if it were Hairball's Great Adventure, instead of Madam's work. Add to this that both pets claim to have special health needs. Frankly, I think they're a couple of hypochondriacs who convinced Madam they must not be left at home with a pet sitter.

All the while Madam drives around Minnesota's hinterlands, showering affection on these pitiful home wreckers, I'm left behind to worry about who pays for my room and next pair of shoes. Mind you, my new farrier, George, has no idea of the financial risk he's running when he comes to see me. I've told him nothing about Madam's current deployment. So far, he continues to show up, so I guess his bills have not yet gone into collection. Nevertheless, since George is a good friend, I'm losing sleep over this matter. Plus, I have many other needs besides shoes—vaccinations, dental appointments, shampoo, hair conditioner, blankets, brushes, and halters ... the list goes on. An attractive fellow such as I needs to keep up with all the current fashion trends as well as designer hair products.

So after pondering the gloomy stream of talk radio plus my limited job prospects, I began to draw up a plan to share with Madam. No more pacing my room, waiting to get bundled off to an animal shelter. Instead, I would apply my talents to a bright new career: writing. Expressing ideas has always been one of my specialties, though certain individuals have called my methods into question. Well, today is a new day. I plan to write a captivating book and use the proceeds to beef up the family treasury. (Um ... "treasury" might be a stretch, but surely I can help support the team, even the hairball benchwarmers.) This new venture might even produce an insurance policy on my home sweet home. Best of all, it strikes me as a fabulous chance to report on some particularly grating human habits and how to retrain them. Maybe I can even teach somebody to change the radio station.

This leads me to a question that probably has occurred to readers: why a book? Not many horses write books. People write books about horses—problem horses, famous horses, horses that break land speed records. Personally, I think humans get carried away writing books about how to fix perfectly fine horses that might have a few unconventional ideas. Yet it has come to my attention that this kind of writing produces income.

Take "natural horsemanship," for instance. Many talented trainers build winning careers writing about natural horsemanship. While this might be a dandy way for humans and horses to get acquainted, I never saw anything so natural about sporting a saddle and Cowboy Bob on my midsection. I mean, how many humans would choose to cart around a fifth grader in a backpack? Of course, I'm used to transporting humans by now but still recall some mishaps during my first human encounters. Okay, how about natural horsemanship from the horse's perspective? Wouldn't that just make a fine subject for me to explore with words?

Speaking of good editorial subjects, I might include a chapter on the horse's art of cultivating human sense. This, of course, directly contradicts the human art of cultivating horse sense. A chapter about this would give me a perfect opportunity to apply my gift for retraining humans. And of course, Madam would make a perfect subject on which to begin.

Now, as for this business about humans with horse sense, I think it's an overrated talent. Well, actually, it's a talent imagined by many humans and achieved by few. For example, if some trainer tries to pry into my personal life with theories about my early childhood development, he probably hasn't taken the time to get to know me. We horses don't misbehave because we have eaten a bad apple. Sometimes, we just don't feel like doing things. Maybe we had a perfectly fine childhood. Maybe we would rather take a little stroll in the woods than join up with some Tom, Dick, or Louise who throws a rope over our head. Humans just need to pay better attention.

So you see, I'm building a case for Noah Vail, the author. Readers might wonder what makes me think I can write books. The seed probably was planted when a misguided racehorse trainer thought he could make a futurity champion out of me. While I certainly know how to run, this fellow's approach never captured my imagination. Hence, we failed to arrive at a common goal. Our business relationship ended one morning when he insisted he'd tried to train me to no avail and stalked off the track, shouting, "Somebody needs to find this blankety-blank horse a job in Ringling Bros. Circus!" I've always felt his outburst was a bit melodramatic, but one must congratulate this lackluster trainer for picking a groovy name for me—Noah Vail.

Along about age two, I met Madam. When I first heard about her, an alarm dinged. It could have been her theological education that made me suspicious. I definitely was not looking for more lessons on the rewards of people pleasing. Or maybe it was the half century she had already spent fiddling around in the horse business. This worried me too. Was she just one more horse jockey planning to teach me new tricks? This also marked my first time partnering with a woman—a *mature* woman, no less. (I believe this is the politically correct term.) No question about it; she came with a boatload of opinions, but I needed a writing partner to actually do the writing. So I decided to park my concerns and take a chance on her.

Let me say right now that it was a good choice. Once Madam and I formally met, I could see she might be my kind of girl after all. And I *do* like girls! In fact, I liked her and all the other Evergreen girls the minute we met outside that muddy stock trailer. What's more, she's turned out to be a good student. If she thought she knew a lot before we met, believe me, she's learned plenty since then. Our chance encounter also has given me an opportunity to develop a few handy training techniques of my own.

Once Madam and I became an item, I discovered she also likes a good adventure. Between the two of us, we have a lot to say about people and the horses that own them. All she really needed was an intelligent horse to observe and conduct interviews. I, on the other hand, needed a partner to manage the transportation, pay the bills, and work the computer keyboard. So our friendship has blossomed into a writing partnership. Whether we produce a human sense manual for horses or a horse sense manual for humans, we figure somebody is bound to gain some sense.

The following stories arose from real (though sometimes embellished) details. Yet in light of today's tendencies toward fictitious memoirs, puffed-up autobiographies, instant rumors, and footloose litigation, I have adjusted names and places wherever it might reflect unfavorably on the author or the management.

So welcome readers. Let me tell you how it all went down ...

2

From Meeker to Maple Plain

They probably heard me well before my personal driver rounded the corner on County Road 6 and rolled into Evergreen Farm. Blessed with a powerful set of pipes, I did my best to notify everyone in the area. I especially liked it when my future friends, dozing in their paddocks, took off bucking at the sound of a new arrival. This is an equine equivalent of "Howdy!" As the big stock trailer rumbled down the driveway, a fresh burst of galloping broke out. Even the neighbor's Angus cattle got in the act. They lumbered in clumsy circles and then rushed the gate to inspect the trailer and its contents. Several of Evergreen's seniors trotted smartly along the fence, demonstrating their best parade horse impersonations. Now, I really could have used a nap after the long drive from Meeker, Oklahoma. Nevertheless, this splendid reception demanded an equally splendid first appearance on my part. If only an esthetician had been on hand to give me a good dusting off and help tidy my hair.

My driver Joe pulled up in front of the barn and stepped out of the truck, where he came face-to-face with a sociable mix of greeters. Call them large, small, round, and tall, with a few dogs and a black barn cat mixed in. They looked like a diversity training class for the American Humane Association. And that didn't include the clutch of women observing us from the barn door. Obviously, this crowd of Minnesotans wanted to take a gander at the handsome beast from Oklahoma. Much as I love attention, my heart started to pound. The waiting throng suddenly looked seriously Scandinavian, blond, and stern. Even though Joe told me it was just my imagination, my initial fervor waned somewhat. I hoped this new partner of mine was standing somewhere in the crowd, preparing to rescue me, should the situation require a rescue. While Joe clattered about, unlatching the tailgate and pulling down the loading ramp, I rehearsed my opening remarks.

Joe already had shared a few details with me about my new partner. He heard through the grapevine that my former trainer had proclaimed I needed to forget racing and find some nice woman to take me in. Frankly, I didn't know what he meant by that. Did he think I was supposed to learn my way around a vacuum and the KitchenAid mixer? Or perhaps he simply meant I would enjoy a new partner. I went with the new partner account, but I did rather like the idea of learning my way around the kitchen. Maybe later.

Anyhoo, Joe also explained that the woman I was about to meet appreciated good horses and treated them well. Yes, yes, we'd all heard that before. But wait—I had to make a valiant attempt to keep a positive attitude. It was, after all, a long hike back to Oklahoma. Joe also attempted to explain how the woman planned to transform me into a dressage competitor. Whoa! That didn't exactly tickle my funny bone. Without meaning to be contrary, let me make it clear that nobody even hinted I might make a good dressage prospect. Boring and tedious came immediately to mind. That didn't even address the distasteful goal of total submission to a rider. Jeez-o-me, I could see we had some educating to do, but it would have to wait. Joe no doubt wanted to get back to Oklahoma. Ready or not, he eased me down the ramp to face the waiting multitude.

The official greeters provided a full representation of the animal kingdom. Even a couple of rabbits watched from their hutch. What a curious place to send a barely ridden, two-year-old horse known for launching jockeys. Yet I must admit, the first welcome warmed this nervous country boy's heart.

"Uh, hello," I mumbled, having already forgotten the rest of my speech.

"Hi to you, cowboy," declared a pint-sized pony named Gilbert. "Welcome to Evergreen Farm."

So far, so good, I thought. They looked hospitable enough, and the Jack Russell terrier showed no sign of grabbing my ankle. Now, which one was Madam? Joe had neglected to tell me her real name, and Madam was the only handle I could come up with. I was anxious to meet her and explain how our new life together would work best, if we focused on writing instead of dressage. She was pretty easy to pick out of the crowd. Hands on her hips, she looked me over as if she were appraising a prospective husband.

I could tell she appreciated my fine physique and elegant mane, not to mention the forelock suavely draped over one eye. That was the best I could do without hair products. *Ah*, I thought, *a woman who appreciates style*. Then she lifted my forelock, looked me straight in the eye, and said, "Welcome to you, partner." Something about the look in her eyes made me think she had been waiting a long time for me to show up.

Now, let me get back to my introduction to Evergreen Farm. First of all, it was clear to me that a guy could get to like this place. A quick inspection revealed a remarkable sight—a horse, to be sure, though a horse that resembled an overstuffed white sofa shambling toward the pasture gate. This expansive silhouette belonged to a Rhinelander gelding, commonly known as a German sport horse. He looked cheery enough, which should not be confused with nimble or sporty. Nor would one describe him as dressage material. This I viewed as a positive development. Miscellaneous greenery hung from his mouth, adding a moose-like quality to the overall picture. A gentle giant like this must do something else for a living. His name was Omar, and he was about to become my pasture partner and best friend.

Omar's partner, Monica, who came to collect him at the gate, qualified as a vision on her own merit. Though he looked like a grass-stained Hindenburg, she cut a tall and stylish figure. She also wore smart-looking riding gear. Madam, on the other hand, was dressed in a peculiar ensemble that combined English and western apparel with a pair of Carhartt boots. While Ms. Monica won top honors for eye appeal, she also dressed Omar in a similar fashion, complete with matching polo wraps and elegant saddle pads. I later learned that Omar was only lukewarm about all the clothing, but this topic was not open for discussion with Monica. Much to my surprise, I also learned that Omar dabbled in dressage and claimed to like it.

So the tour began. No question—Evergreen featured tip-top services, including comfy rooms, lots of windows, and two water buckets—one for washing my hay and one for sipping. Most important, every room had a card table. Canasta, gin rummy, five-card draw—you name it; they played it here. Tack rooms even included cribbage boards and jigsaw puzzles. The spa looked inviting, with plenty of hair-care products. The pastures offered shady corners for rest and relaxation. Best of all, the place was designed for easy visiting with neighbors. I especially liked the open view of all the action in the aisles and arenas. Overall, it felt pretty darn homey. All I needed was a bit of time to point Madam down the right career track.

The first week passed smoothly, with just one small mix-up. It took the landlord a few attempts to get me settled in the ideal room. The first try lit my fire of fondness for females. I happen to enjoy the company of attractive members of the opposite sex, both human and equine. What a thrill it was to learn that my new neighbor, a lovely bay mare named Faith, resided directly across from me. It must have been that special sway of her hips that piqued my interest. Or it was her luminous dark eyes that caused my heart to flutter. Either way, I wasted no time cooking up a little romantic tête-à-tête between our stalls. Faith merely rolled her eyes and looked out the window. I even tried sharing some of my second-cut alfalfa, but that did not light her fire either. She persisted playing hard to get, though I think she really fell for me and just refused to admit it. In any case, dear Faith must have filed a complaint with the landlord, because the next thing I knew, they moved me to a new spot, next to a guy named Copper.

Copper's early career included stints at racetracks across the country. We shared some good gossip about trainers and famous horses we had met. Then, for no reason, he turned a little moody on me. The landlord then invited me to test yet another room. This revolving room exercise was getting embarrassing. After all, I was practicing my best stable etiquette, but the landlord insisted I talked too much. Then I was placed next to a variation of a draft horse named Patrick. At least he liked to play gin rummy and didn't mind listening to a few racetrack stories. Landlord number one (there were two) might have saved herself a lot of time and trouble if she had used one of those online roommate-matching services.

Did I mention that I like cats? There were three barn cats at Evergreen, hanging around the grooming area, exchanging recipes for mole fricassee and sautéed sparrow. It looked to me as if only one of those felines understood a barn cat's job description—catching mice. The other two lay around discussing the prospect of catching mice, though I had yet to see any follow-up. Fang, a gray male, came equipped with oversized incisors that hung below his lips. One would think his vampire looks would cause mice to fall over in a faint, but Fang never even thought about hunting. He did, however, recline regularly on my backside. Wicked, a plumpish female, piddled in the landlord's tack trunks. This resulted in a lot of shrieking from anybody who witnessed the offense.

Last was Snuggles. During my first week at Evergreen, I stood in the grooming stall, quietly waiting for Madam to show up with a saddle. The two lazy cats were holding court and doing little else. Suddenly, Snuggles came through the front door like a heat-seeking missile. She was gaining on a fast chipmunk. The other two cats and I watched with some interest, until Snuggles and the chipmunk made a sharp U-turn in the aisle and headed back our way. The lazy cats took flight, though I couldn't locate their escape route. Then, for no particular reason, the chipmunk made a banking turn into the grooming stall and sped right up my back leg. Snuggles commenced to bat at the chipmunk until I was forced to intervene. The chipmunk escaped without injury and without causing me bodily harm. Snuggles, on the other hand, didn't speak to me for a week.

Each day, my orientation produced something unusual, so it should not have surprised me when I discovered they called this place a horse establishment, even though some kind of woodworking activity buzzed away in a shop located directly behind my room. It was called Wally's Woodworking, and its president, a portly Jack Russell terrier named Wally, could have passed as a small version of Omar. He was white and shaped like a loaf of bread. Wally manufactured custom-built horse show products, including tack trunks, saddle racks, and an occasional bluebird house. He must have employed some help, because he wasn't tall enough to run much more than a jigsaw. Besides, he couldn't possibly see over the steering wheel to ferry packages to and from the Mound post office. Actually, I suspect Wally got a little help from Mr. and Mrs. Landlord—both wore aprons decorated in marine varnish and sawdust.

Fortunately, I do not suffer from sleep problems, because whenever Wally got a large order, his shop sounded like the Oshkosh Air Show. Saws whined. Mr. and Mrs. Landlord loudly expressed themselves above the din. Doors slammed. Suffice it to say nobody entered Wally's Woodworking until they saw the completed order heading down the road to the post office. Wally's newest creation, a memory box, caused quite a stir among his customers. He told us this little beauty, complete with handsome brass fittings, also passed as a horse casket. Who would have thought such an attractive item would accommodate the ashes of a full-sized horse? The boxes became so popular that one of the local farriers ordered a jazzy version for himself and another for his wife.

A couple of introductory weeks and a delectable menu found me settling comfortably into my new Minnesota home. Even Evergreen's companion goat, Bella, fit right in. Madam and I got off to a polite start, though we had not yet discussed this new writing career of mine. We hadn't exactly worked our way through the dressage career conversation either. Meanwhile, Omar already was taking orders well, and he was generous with his horse treats. In fact, everyone at Evergreen carried pockets full of treats. This too added a cheery note to the day.

3

Madam and Noah Sign
an Author's Agreement

Madam and I needed to talk. Actually, we needed to come
to an understanding about our goals as they related to writing a book.
Generally speaking, we came to agreement on our individual tasks. A few
details remained to be discussed, such as the radio that interrupted my
rest and my creative processes and train of thought.

That confounded thing was at it again. Once both landlords,
agreed on my permanent room location, I figured the radio problem
would get resolved, but the thing sat on a shelf right outside my newest
room. I planned to take action—what a perfect opportunity to set the dial
permanently on jazz. If Holstein cattle gave more milk with soft jazz
accompaniment, imagine what it could do for those of us fledging
authors. It also occurred to me that a little well-placed rubber cement
might prevent any future dial tampering. Well, that's what I thought
anyway. It later came to my attention that someone slipped in and

cranked the cemented knob to one of those nasty natter talk stations. I wouldn't complain about neighborly talk radio—the kind that announces Pet Palooza or lunch specials at the Dew Drop Inn. It was the hosts who churned out insults and conspiracy theories that got to me. It also kept me awake. As a card-carrying ambassador of civil discourse, the rant brigade left me with just one choice—turn it off and invite someone over for dinner.

The sneaky switch from Norah Jones to terrible twaddle also caused my newest neighbor Patrick to break out in hives. That prompted speculation about whether he had eaten a pepperoni pizza or taken a nap in poison oak. He might have done both. His partner, Katherine, jumped into action. She'd been dialing up the University of Minnesota's Large Animal Clinic for the past two days, trying to get a handle on Patrick's lumps. The poor guy was put on prednisone and bed rest. Unlike yours truly, Patrick had not yet enrolled in speech class. Hence, nobody understood him or offered much sympathy when he tried to explain that the radio caused his problem. For Pete's sake, the darn thing blasted directly into his left ear. Patrick and I barely had become acquainted; we'd just started to enjoy a bit of congenial dinner conversation, followed by a quiet game of Scrabble—and now this.

Well, all this brings me back to my business meeting with Madam. She arrived wearing a smile and carrying a bag of carrots— always a good conversation starter. Unfortunately, she began with some sort of a homily about the grand new journey we were about to take together. It seemed a little cliché, but I kept my own counsel while she exercised her lips. "New"—yes, as not many horses take up a literary career with their humans. "Journey"—I'm not so sure. That sounded like a lot of deep thinking or discovering new galaxies. Granted, our undertaking might be unusual but it felt more like an expedition, an excursion across the country, meeting new friends and broadening our horizons. It also was about testing the boundaries of horse and human partnerships. Journey just sounded a little too New Age-y.

She then produced a single sheet of paper with our names written at the top. "I thought we could start by signing an author's agreement," she announced.

"Well, that depends on what we are agreeing on," I replied

cautiously.

That was easy enough—I'd talk; she'd type. I'd train; she'd learn. I'd travel; she'd drive. I supposed it wouldn't hurt to sign an official agreement over such things.

So she showed it to me.

"Hmm ... this covers a few interesting ground rules," I suggested. "Fairness matters. Kindness wins the day. Friendship at all cost, and fun at every opportunity."

My goodness, nobody ever had asked me to sign something like this. It all looked straightforward and agreeable, but I was not quite ready to put my John Hancock on the dotted line. Instead, I decided to report the radio dilemma and tell her how it threatened to wreck Patrick's and my dinner. "Plus, I can't write or think straight under such conditions," I declared.

Madam listened thoughtfully, and then she stood up without a word. I held my breath, waiting for her response and hoping she didn't find my complaint too bold.

"I have the answer," she announced as she took off out the front door to her car. A few minutes later, she returned with two small boxes, one for Patrick and the other for me.

"Look, iPods!" I shouted to Patrick.

With that, she unplugged the radio and took it away. That's when I officially signed on the dotted line, and we commenced to write our masterpiece together.

4
Never Say Neigh

I love the word yes. Yes rings of escapades. It feels like a path to new things and exciting possibilities. In my opinion, too much *no* creates needless anxiety and missed opportunities. I'm speaking from my own experience, as I used to say no to everything. No bath. No plastic bag flapping around me. No trailer rides. And for Pete's sake, no winter blankets. Not only have I missed a boatload of treats and chances to go places, but I spent a couple of mighty nippy winters wearing nothing but my skivvies. So when Madam told me her story about her first horse, I was glad to hear it was a *yes* kind of story. Well, yes to almost everyone except maybe Mrs. Langford, though truthfully, even she came out better—or at least a little better informed about girls and their horses. The story goes like this:

Madam managed to win over her parents when it came to horses. By this, I mean her mother and father admitted defeat early and bought her a horse named Koko. Now, I never met Koko, but she sounded like she came up short in the good manners department. Madam, though, saw nothing less than perfection and dependable transportation to her friend Robin Langford's house. Robin had a horse too. Together, the girls nearly wore out their horses. Some days, they saddled up early and came home late. They trotted cross-country and around town, dressed like Roy Rogers, ready to lasso a stray cat. Madam dolled up Koko's mane and tail with rose oil hair tonic from the local drugstore. The girls blackened their horses' hooves with boot polish and painted diamond shapes on the horses' rumps.

Some days they hung around the backyard, inspecting their horses, pretending to be show judges. They bragged about their horses' bloodlines, though neither knew much about bloodlines. Other days, they galloped around the neighborhood, posing as King Arthur or Chief Seattle. The girls taught their horses to jump barrels and fallen trees and took them swimming in Lowes Creek. They worked hard at inventing ways to play with their horses. Most of what Madam described sounded like fun, except for the part about lassoing cats.

Robin also had two Shetland ponies named Cindy and Midge. Every so often, Cindy gave birth to a foal about the size of a cocker spaniel. Nobody could explain this little marvel of birth, as no stallion ponies lived in the area. Sometimes the girls dressed the ponies in circus costumes and hitched them to a wagon. Neither Cindy nor Midge liked that much, which didn't surprise me. Shetland ponies tend to bristle at basic pony activities, such as wearing saddles and bridles or ferrying girls on their backs shouting, "Yahoo!" Midge usually ran off with her rider or plunged her head down to graze at an inopportune moment. This resulted in the saddle falling over Midge's neck, causing her rider to land face first in the sand burs. Cindy enjoyed rolling in the dirt, a trick that caused serious wear and tear, both on saddles and riders.

One time, according to Madam, she and Robin convinced Robin's horse, Sherry, to come into the Langfords' kitchen. Perhaps this crossed the line in terms of healthy horseplay, though I admit I've enjoyed time in offices and tack rooms posted as "No horses allowed." In any case, the girls had little chance to applaud their success coaxing

Sherry up the steps and in the back door. No sooner had they led her through the mudroom into the kitchen than Robin's mother returned home from a bridge game. Bargaining with Sherry about hurrying out the back door looked like a bad plan. So Robin put some cereal on the stovetop to keep Sherry occupied while the girls worked on an escape route. Unfortunately for everybody, Mrs. Langford sashayed into the kitchen before any such plan materialized. I do wish I'd been there to watch when she poked her head around the refrigerator and beheld the view. Both girls ducked into the mudroom, leaving Sherry munching Cheerios off the stovetop.

No surprise that Mrs. Langford's screams startled Sherry. This launched a series of events that alerted the fire department and dismantled the Langfords' kitchen. The small space hardly allowed for Sherry to run for cover. She did, however, jump on the open dishwasher door. She also collided with the stove, knocking a good bit of cookware to the floor. All this resulted in Sherry's slipping on the linoleum floor and nearly trampling everyone. Details of what happened next remain unclear, but I understand everyone, including the horse, escaped without injury. Mrs. Langford, never warmed to the humor of the situation, but she did appreciate her new dishwasher and redecorated kitchen. Sherry learned quite a bit, including how to navigate steps and eat breakfast cereal off a stovetop. The girls received a severe reprimand for their antics but recovered quickly. It seemed to me that everybody gained a little something from this creative exploit.

"Horse crazy," their parents called them. No piano lessons, no summer camp, no party dresses—at age ten, Robin and Madam thought of nothing but horses and all adventures they could experience with their horses. This passion for everything horse furnished the backdrop for the arrival of a new neighbor.

Shortly after the kitchen incident, Madam's mother reported that a man with racehorses had moved in next door. Madam wasted no time getting to the phone to share this good news with Robin. The only thing more exciting than their own horses was meeting someone who actually raced horses. In fact, Madam had already decided she planned to be a jockey, so this fit well into her training. One small observation on my part: this new neighbor faced a daunting task if he thought he could keep these girls out of his life. First, however, Madam had to figure out how to meet the guy—but she was a child who showed no signs of shyness. She jumped into her new Tony Lama boots, strapped on a favorite Gene Autry belt, and trotted over to meet the new neighbor, Bob Stall. (A fitting name, don't you think?)

According to Madam, the sagging barn was a bit disappointing. Daylight streamed through the unpainted boards. Pink hollyhocks poked between an empty corncrib and a crumbling cement silo. Holes near the barn's foundation hinted of rats—or worse. *A pretty seedy place*, Madam thought, *but maybe this fellow has a property improvement plan*. In any case, she saw no sign of the racehorse man, so she tiptoed around the decaying shed. Suddenly, a voice shot out, "Get the hell off my property!" She did exactly that.

This was not going to be easy, but she concluded it simply required a new tack.

The next day, she waited until late in the afternoon, when the old man left the barn for home. Once his car rattled out the driveway, she slipped across the pasture and into the tumbledown barn. Armed with her Labrador retriever, Sam, Madam let her eyes adjust to the darkness. She stepped into a small feed room that smelled of molasses and alfalfa. Two horses peered curiously from their box stalls as she crept into the main section of the barn. The place looked modest but tidy. A grooming box next to the stalls held brushes of all shapes, hoof picks, and sweat scrapers. A stack of clean towels, buckets, saddle soap, and assorted syringes and veterinary products neatly lined the shelves. But harnesses, not saddles, hung on the wall. The smell of oiled leather filled her nostrils as she picked through a pile of horseshoes, an old farrier's apron, and several large fly nets. A picture on the wall said "Dan Patch" beneath it. Torn by a temptation to explore further and her dread of getting caught, she quickly glanced at the unusual-looking horses and darted out through the same door she'd entered.

For the next few days, Madam watched the old man through her mother's binoculars, but eventually, his morning workouts lured her closer. She stole through the trees and hid under some small jack pines near the edge of his exercise track. To her surprise, he owned harness racing horses, not saddle horses—two fine-looking geldings. One was a trotter and the other a pacer. He worked each horse every morning. Madam said she laid low and listened to the rhythmic breathing as their hooves pounded the track. Nostrils flared from powerful breathing, their chests dripped white lather. The veins on their necks protruded beneath glistening streams of sweat. As the sulky wheels spun along the dirt track, the ground exploded with little puffs of dust. She could hear the pacer's hobbles slap against his legs. Thrilling or not, common sense told Madam to stay under cover.

Later, Madam would learn more details about these special horses. They were called Standardbreds, a breed that combined the blood of three breeds, the thoroughbred, the Morgan, and the Narragansett Pacer. The *standard* referred to a 2:30 minute mark, under which a horse had to trot or pace one mile. Standardbreds raced under harness and played a colorful role in the history of American horseracing. An English thoroughbred named Messenger became the foundation sire of this breed. Following the Civil War, his great-grandson sired more than 1,300 foals that dominated harness racing.

All of us horses can trot, so I sort of understood Madam when she explained how a trotter moves its legs diagonally, right front and left hind and then left front and right hind striking the ground simultaneously. But pacing sounded a little complicated. A pacer moves its legs laterally, right front and right hind and then left front and left hind striking the ground simultaneously. She said some horses, such as Standardbreds, get good at it and can really fly. That's the part that interested me—speed. I might not know how to pace but after hearing this story, I intended to add harness racing to my bucket list.

Madam's story continued with the old man discovering her as she watched him from her hideout. Again, he bellowed at her with a fierceness that sent her scampering for home. Frankly, I could already tell that by the end of her story, she would wear this guy down, but for the time being, she just watched the old horseman, with his deeply lined face and powerful hands that held the reins almost daintily. He wore bib overalls and spoke quietly to the horses. *He may not like me*, she thought, *but he sure loves those horses*. Again and again, she returned to watch, curious about the gentleness and skill of this grumpy hermit.

"When he finished working one horse, he led it back to the barn, removed the harness, and bathed the sweaty animal with a vinegar and liniment mix in warm water," Madam explained. "Then he repeated the same process with the second. Finally, he cleaned them off with a sweat scraper and wrapped their legs in long white bandages. It took all morning for him to complete the exercise routines and return the horses to their freshly bedded stalls."

About noon, she said, he swept the barn aisle, removed his overalls, and hung them on a wooden peg. Then the barn fell silent for a couple of hours while he napped. Finally, he drove off down the road to his home.

After watching this process for about two weeks, Madam mustered the courage to try a new approach. This time, she rode Koko over to his place, convinced he couldn't reach her with those huge hands as long as she stayed on the horse. As she approached the track, he led the pacer up the drive in her direction. She waited, frightened and frozen in his path. He simply walked around her without speaking. At the edge of the track, he hooked up the overcheck, adjusted the blinkers, and climbed into the sulky.

The horse moved off at a walk and eventually into a moderate pace. Dust rolled off the sulky wheels. The silver spokes whirled in the sunlight as if moving in both directions at once. The gelding glided effortlessly over the track. Only the bobble of his head indicated he was putting out any effort. After several minutes pacing at a measured speed, the old man pulled up on the reins and reversed his direction on the track. Immediately, the gelding surged forward at a racing gait. The tempo of clopping hooves increased, showering the old man's goggles with fine sand. Most people would have made a safe exit at that point, but not Madam. She waited.

After completing the workout, the man walked the horse twice around the track to cool him out. Then, he returned to the driveway, where Madam sat on a now fidgeting Koko, who'd lost interest in this visit shortly after the first trip around the track.

"What's yer name?" he grunted, climbing out of the sulky and releasing the overcheck.

"Mary," replied Madam.

"Okay, Marian, if you're so blessed interested in what I do around here, climb down off that old goat and cool this one out."

Madam slipped from the saddle and tied Koko to a tree. The man buckled a halter on the gelding and handed her the lead rope. The simple exchange marked the beginning of an unlikely friendship with the old horseman named Bob Stall. The two eventually would share a small world of oats, liniment, and horse-racing memories from years past. Madam said she learned about Dan Patch, a pacer who set a record for running a quarter-mile in one minute, fifty-five seconds as a nine-year-old. The record lasted for thirty-two years. Old Bob talked about the great horse Hambletonian and the Hambletonian Stake, a famous race that began at the New York State Fair in 1926.

Bob eventually agreed to shoe Koko and taught Madam how to care for horses properly. He drove her and Robin to the Chippewa County Fairground harness racing stable to meet his only friend, George Ashe. The two of them talked about trading horses in Fort Dodge, Iowa, and winning races in Milwaukee and Michigan. Robin and Madam sat on a tack trunk, listening to wild tales about runaways on the racetrack, overturned sulkies, and screaming fans.

At first, nobody believed that old Bob let the girls come onto his property. He had a reputation for running people out of his barn and out of his life. The girls didn't know that. They couldn't get enough of his stories about grandstand calamities and racetrack speed records. As for his own geldings, he said they once had been great prospects at the track until one suffered from a life-threatening puncture wound in his chest by running into a metal fence post. The other horse shin-bucked during his early training, causing an injury of the canon bone that ended his racing career. The puncture wound required months of care and ultimately left a jagged scar. In both cases, the geldings required more rehabilitation than their trainers chose to invest, so Bob took them home with him. Madam never learned whether he later raced them again or simply enjoyed their company.

Robin and Madam stumbled into the world of an unsuspecting old horseman; Bob Stall ran headlong into two horse-crazy ten-year-olds. His horses comprised his circle of friends. Old photos and newspaper clippings provided his only social contact. Their unusual friendship, which began through a mutual love of horses, offered a bright human connection for a solitary old fellow who finally said yes.

Years later, Madam would have an opportunity to drive roadster horses (harness horses spiffed up for the show ring). Thanks to Bob, she remembered how to put a harness on right side up and drive around a track without causing a wreck. Many years after that, I would benefit from what she learned.

"Once you choose to bring a horse into your trust and care, you must continue to provide that trust and care in sickness or injury," Bob had told her. Mostly, though, I think Madam learned from him how to just hang out with me.

5

More Revolving Rooms

I liked my newest room. It took long enough for the landlord to quit playing musical bed-and-board and decide where to put me. Actually, it took both landlords, debating my locale in high-pitched voices, to complete the transaction. But in the end I must give them credit for making such a wise choice. *Voila*! My final relocation plan snapped into place, and there I was in a sparkling new room. This one offered the best of several amenities—a perfect spot for good viewing and ideal for greeting guests, and practical for conducting face-to-face interviews.

I also was delighted to have a superb view of Faith, that heavenly creature who continued to play hard-to-get. This new living arrangement allowed me to observe her long eyelashes and lovely face morning, noon and night. While it was possible I welcomed this development more eagerly than did Faith, I planned to exercise the utmost patience in winning her affection. It was just a matter of time before she discovered I was simply irresistible.

I was excited to be near the front door, where most daily proceedings began. Morning usually commenced with Wally, of Wally's Woodworking fame, parading across the driveway and into our lobby. He tended to hold forth, chastising barn swallows and imagined mice, which involved more barking than necessary, I might add. Anyone who knows a Jack Russell terrier knows the meaning of "in charge." Not that I dislike Jack Russells. In my book, they get an A for their human management skills. Wally, for example, would sit in the driver's seat of his own business. As a company CEO, he singlehandedly ran a successful woodworking business that hummed along, turning out orders and delivering paychecks. With the assistance of two employees—the landlords of whom I just spoke—he produced an impressive line of items popular with show jumpers and racehorses.

That morning, Wally showed up dressed in a plaid jacket that hugged his ample frame like a peel hugs a banana. As an Evergreen newcomer, I avoided any mention of this upholstered look. I thought perhaps he and I could discuss style at a later date. Wally claimed to work half-days operating a jigsaw. Word had it that he really did little more than direct the help and scold the cats before returning indoors to enjoy a cup of tea and a nap on the couch.

Next in the door came one of several veterinarians looking for a patient. Like it or not, that patient almost always landed in the grooming stall next to me. I appreciated this. It gave me a good seat to observe all procedures without enduring the discomfort of pokes in my privates. Often during the vet's visit, a big fellow operating a front-end loader would stick his head in the door to inquire where to stack hay. Patrick would tell me he'd been delivering hay here for a decade. I think he just liked to chat up our attractive female vet or to make sure someone brought a box of doughnuts to go with his coffee.

A retired mechanic also came to call about once a week to see what needed fixing. Mr. Landlord hid from him, claiming he was a mechanical disaster who periodically started a fire or drove over Mrs. Landlord's tomato plants. In fact, Mr. Landlord parked an old wreck of a tractor behind the barn to keep this neighborly mechanic busy without causing an explosion.

Then there was Duane, the dentist. I don't usually care for dentistry, but Duane did something different. He practiced voodoo— at least, he cast spells, because all the horses liked him. Duane ran a bare-bones operation—nothing more than a cell phone, a pickup truck, and what looked like a few kitchen utensils. No big box of anesthesia and wrenches. No medieval mouth speculums. No needles or laughing gas. He didn't even wear one of those miner's lights on his head for peering down a horse's throat. It was just plain Duane, wearing a baseball cap and a big grin.

Duane whistled a lot. He would come and go around the barn, visiting every pony and retired pasture pet, whistling show tunes along the way. Just when I thought an uncooperative guy like Prince might flatten him, Duane convinced Prince that his world was about to become a better place due to a dental appointment with Duane. Every horse in the place opened up and said *ah*, the minute they saw Duane shambling down the aisle. When he was done polishing their choppers, they all thanked him for taking the trouble. It was a mystery.

My new room provided excellent viewing of Duane, among other things. My latest neighbors included Gabe, the resident cribbage professional. Gabe spent hours online, playing Words with Friends and studying cribbage CliffsNotes. He rarely lost a game—another mystery. Gabe was the first equine card shark I ever met.

Another new acquaintance, Bella the milking goat, spent her time with a foxy thoroughbred mare named Olivia. They made an unusual couple. Olivia might not have been my kind of girl, but she was a looker. Actually, Madam just had a tête-à-tête with her that cooled my flirting tendencies. It began when Andres, our director of housekeeping, asked Madam to help him catch Olivia. Olivia, however, showed little interest in getting caught. Instead, the instant Madam stepped into the paddock with a halter and rope, Olivia charged her. This sent Madam diving under the fence. Apparently, Madam viewed Olivia's move as throwing down the gauntlet. She dusted herself off, set her jaw, and marched back in the arena, swinging a rope in circles above her head. I was afraid to watch. The galloping Olivia, the twirling rope—it was a frightening sight, and it cooled any ardor I might have initially nursed for Olivia. Fortunately, this event came to a peaceful end, with Olivia following Madam out the gate like a pet poodle. I turned my longing gaze back to Faith.

While Evergreen offered a good selection of horse entertainment, the best part about my new room was that it let me supervise the barn farriers, the guys who managed our shoe department. Just that morning, I'd enjoyed my first taste of farrier day. It began early, with a rumpus room full of young girls galloping past my room. Of course, they galloped because they pretended to be horses. All girls ages ten and under pretend to be horses. Today, they came for horse camp … and perhaps to learn a little something about shoeing horses. So far, it looked more like a tutorial in how not to groom and bridle a pony.

Anyhoo, farrier day refers to the day when those no-nonsense chaps pay Evergreen a visit. Farriers rule, in my estimation. Horses famous for mashing toes and breaking halters change their tune when a farrier shows up. Even the nibblers stand quietly. My guy, George, would tell you I've never so much as tweaked his back pocket for a mint when he gives me a pedicure. Actually, farriers aren't big on mints or any other horse treats, but they do know how to manage small campers who gallop up and down the aisle, pretending to be horses. They're efficient, civil, and they get their work done without a fuss. Farriers probably should be running for school boards or governor somewhere.

Now, I can't speak from experience about female farriers, but the guys make up a sturdy social club of plain-speaking horsemen. It should come as no surprise that prima donna warmblood horses, fond of leaning and knocking over tool boxes, don't appeal much to farriers. This is where my new room got interesting. I got to observe the progress that takes place when a prima donna warmblood met a farrier. After a few appointments, even the problem children came to attention when they saw a shoe guy step through the door. Omar, for example, the consummate butt nibbler, behaved like a West Point cadet when his farrier, Mark, showed up. Omar, masquerading as a large dressage sofa, dwarfed Mark, who weighed in at about 134 pounds. It's important to note here that size does not enjoy an advantage in the horseshoeing stall; farriers do.

Years of traveling from one stable to another gave farriers a jump-start on local gossip. They always knew who paid too much for a top-notch horse, or who left town with someone else's brother-in-law. They also kept excellent records on who got fired or who overdid the liquid refreshments at a garden party and fell in the swimming pool. A discerning farrier with a good ear could tell the *National Enquirer* a thing or two. Yet they tended to keep important rumors and memorable scandals to themselves and their best clients. They also knew how to tell a good story. This was why I quickly learned to keep a notepad handy on farrier day.

Shortly after settling in at Evergreen, a farrier named Roy stopped in to do a little work on Gabe's feet. This guy barely picked up his apron and a box of nails before he began telling the landlords a little tale about a recent incident involving an anvil—that's the heavy steel apparatus used to shape horseshoes. Well, Roy began by explaining how he had spent a long day shoeing horses down in the southern part of the state. After hours of hard labor, he packed up his truck and started the three-hour drive home. This drive took him north on Highway 61, which runs along the Mississippi River. A stream of traffic trailed behind him as he drove at a modest speed through Wabasha and Lake City. Drivers were becoming more impatient as they motored up and down the long hills, all the time chugging along behind Roy. Nobody could find a place to pass. Roy made no effort to move onto the shoulder and let them go around him. Eventually, the driver directly behind him started to tailgate. Then someone honked his horn. Then another honked. Roy started to get agitated.

He began to hum a few Broadway tunes to settle his nerves. That didn't help, so he started to make a mental list of all the thoughts he would like to share with the tailgater, should they get a chance to meet. Meanwhile, the heavy load in the back of his truck did not allow him to drive any faster, nor was he inclined to stop on a hill and discuss particulars with the offending driver. He continued ignoring the honkers and moseyed along the best he could. Eventually, the traffic started to thin. Then, rather abruptly, it disappeared. To Roy's relief, the long trail of cars and recreational vehicles either turned off in search of a restaurant or just evaporated into the deepening evening darkness.

Pretty soon, Roy arrived in the city of Hastings, where he thought it might be a good time to stop for a piece of apple pie. He pulled in at a favorite truck stop, got out of his truck, and walked to the back to check out everything before heading in to order. That's when he noticed the back door of his camper was not properly latched. It reminded him that he should start locking his truck if he planned to do so much traveling. A quick inventory of his shoeing tools revealed that he had left his anvil at the stable, where he had been working all day. *Drat*, he thought—he'd have to drive back the next morning to pick it up.

It took two cups of coffee and a piece of pie à la mode before Roy realized he had *not* left his anvil at the stable. Furthermore, he might know why that long line of traffic magically disappeared from behind him. He finished his coffee and drove back to the hill where he had suddenly parted company with the traffic. No anvil—but wherever it landed, it must have been exciting for the drivers behind him.

Finding the anvil required another story. It took Roy many months to figure out where the anvil had come to rest. It took even longer to track down the couple that drove home with it stuck in the grille of their SUV. At that point, Roy decided to make an offer on the bent-up lump of steel that currently passed as the couple's garden art. However, he chose not to share the anvil's history with the couple. Instead, he paid nearly five hundred dollars to buy it back.

"I collect anvils," said Roy with a hint of a smile. "And sometimes, circumstances force a fellow to buy his own anvil more than once."

6

Hooray for Mud Season

Call it what you will—global warming, meteorologist nightmare, political hot potato, or climate change—but with all the changeable weather and the help of some heavy downpours, it has turned into that delightful time of year: mud season! It arrived rather abruptly and without warning. Omar insisted it also came a month early, but I wouldn't know that, coming from Oklahoma, where weather operates without a schedule. According to my new friend and tour guide Omar, just a week or so ago, he and the crew were skijoring around the neighborhood, confident they still had weeks of winter sports ahead of them. Skijoring, I learned, usually involves dogs powering cross-country skiers behind them at the end of a long rope. Omar perfected a similar technique for Evergreen's horses, though I suspect it does not involve much powering. In any case, skijoring season ground to a halt when the temperature shot up to 70 degrees. *Voila*—Evergreen morphed into a spring swill, just in time for my arrival. (Honestly, it's hard not to love a word like swill!)

Omar also told me that Minnesota winters used to behave like winter. Everybody's garden hose would freeze up by Thanksgiving. Then a couple feet of snow would fall. After that, the entire state's population augured in for the longest season of the year. This was accompanied by grievances about the weather until May.

"This winter, though," Omar said, "couldn't seem to get started. We occasionally heard radio warnings about a 'Snowmageddon' event coming our way, but it never happened."

I was starting to see a pattern in this non-winter he talked about. First, the TV weather predictor forecasted an incoming storm the size of Brazil that was lurking in the Rocky Mountains. Next came a run on grocery stores, as if sustenance might never again appear in our region. Following that, Evergreen's landlords bundled off to the Maple Plain Co-Op to top up our groceries. Soon enough, the weather predictor forecasted that the storm had changed direction and would take out Chicago by nightfall. It might rain. The wind might blow 70 miles per hour, or the temperature might drop below zero. Or not. All or none of those weather elements could overtake the Midwest by morning. This was the time when Horseopoly games and jigsaw puzzles started turning up in the lunchroom, according to Omar. Card tables suddenly appeared, and the Bob Dylan music played on. Frankly, this was starting to sound a bit like Oklahoma weather, though the addition of cards and board games was a nice touch.

None of this weather disarray would matter, except from what I hear, it wreaked havoc with the Evergreen hoofleball field. One day, the boys played on rock-hard ground with no snow. The next day, the temps rose, it poured icy-cold rain, and everything turned to muck. Finally, they got just enough snow to transform the field into a luge track. Fortunately, nobody suffered any serious falls, though Clyde the Belgian hoofleball goalie had to catch a few Evergreen oldsters before they took headers on the ice. (Good grief, we will have to speak to the TV weather predictor before next winter rolls around.)

All that consternation over climate upset has passed; now I'm speaking of mud. Oh, joy! It arrived very early and looked as if it might stick around. For those unlucky souls who never enjoyed the marvels of mud, let me explain. First, it comes in assorted types. Mudpacks, mud wrestling, mud baths, and mud pies. Mud provides both therapeutic and cosmetic improvements. None of this excites me, however, as much as the mud just inside our pasture gate—the pleasingly squishy spot that yesterday served as the hoofleball goal. Last night's rain added good texture to a fabulous mud hole for everybody to enjoy. In fact, after Omar and I gave it a test run, we planned to send out invitations to the neighbors to stop in for a bit of mud therapy!

Spring mud arrives at a perfect time. Mud declares the end of short days and long nights. It proclaims relief from all this itchy hair stuck under soiled winter blankets that have held us prisoner for months. Even in Oklahoma, mud season means it's time for every self-respecting horse to take a swan dive in the sludge. Of course, one cannot overlook the restorative benefits of such a dive. Frankly, mud might be equally therapeutic for humans. Mud can fix every sort of rash and grumble. It takes away the sting of small affronts and bad poker hands. It certainly helps with gnat management, if you happen to be a horse. Mud soothes and refreshes. It puts life back in balance and offers a great sense of freedom after long months bundled up in a seemingly bulletproof horse rug. I admit, restrictive garments are not my style, so I'm thrilled to say adios to that itchy straight jacket I've been wearing.

Best of all, mud never fails to prompt a shriek from Madam. I love the way she sprints for the vacuum and cleaning supplies whenever I return to my room, sporting a suit of clay and a halter stuck to my head. Armed with shedding blades and hair-detangling goo she lectures me on the values of cleanliness. (Yeah right. Just like we all know the value of a colonoscopy and getting our eyebrows waxed! Fine ideas for someone, though neither would top my to-do list.)

I've been thinking of other possible mud benefits. I'd bet a good scrub in the muck could cut down on bullying incidents. Or a reckless cannonball in the slop might even help manage road rage, or promote a degree of civility in the legislative process and on certain call-in radio shows. How about offering a mud hole as an employment benefit? Wouldn't that be swell? One look at the Evergreen crew returning to the barn tells me they too have enjoyed a seasonal attitude adjustment thanks to our spring mud. We all have!

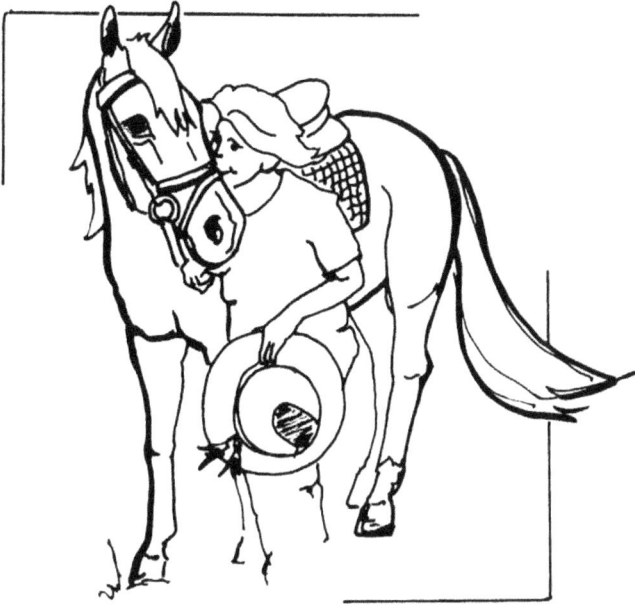

7

A Strange Encounter in Baker Park

Now that Madam and I had ironed out our business arrangements—I talk, she types—it was time to get out and take in the local sights. One thing I already appreciated about Madam was that she encouraged me to use my own mind. She liked to toss me a new learning opportunity and then let me figure out how to get it right. Most of the time, this method worked, though now and again, not perfectly. Such was the day we set out on one of our first trail rides in Baker Park. That was the time we managed to clear the park of any freelance Rollerbladers.

It all began innocently enough on a flawless spring afternoon. A fresh burst of plum blossoms, migrating Canada geese, and the smell of first-crop alfalfa made a perfect setting for exploring a new trail. Madam's and my partnership had improved following a couple of minor missteps early on—like our first trip out when I trod upon a springy tree branch that snapped me in my boy parts. This resulted in a few "airs above the ground" (a quaint dressage term referring to an elevated leap). Some uncalled-for remarks from our riding group followed. Apparently, Madam's backside rising above the saddle caused an overreaction from the others. I did speak to her about finding me a western stock saddle for our trail riding, but advice from the horse often gets lost in translation. Anyhoo, all ended well, literally. Madam's derrière ended up squarely in the middle of her Kiefer dressage saddle, none the worse for wear. This caused quite a jolt for me, but we both recovered our balance and trotted on.

A second little fuss took place a week ago when we met a mother woodcock. This stumpy bird sported a bill like a dagger and an eye for combat. It launched into an alarming dance that surprised me so that I landed in a plum thicket. (By the way, horses often have strong feelings about bird tricks. This includes wild turkeys flopping in the underbrush or squawking pheasants making a run for it across the trail!)

And then there was the encounter with a bloated raccoon carcass. Such an odor, I've never smelled! That thing looked like a bad fur hat. The situation also convinced Madam to step off and walk around the offending item. Good of her to give me time to gather my wits. Though these initial lapses in bravery seemed small, they caused a stern lecture from Madam.

"I intend to own a bomb-proof horse one day, Noah," she intoned. "With or without you!" Not especially comforting language from a brand new partner.

Fortunately, our small calamities passed without serious damage, and our life together on the trail improved. Today promised a relaxing afternoon communing with nature. That's precisely how it went until we reached a point somewhere between the public port-a-potty and the Three Rivers Park dog-walking rules. We were enjoying a smart gallop through the woods when it happened. A human of some order magically appeared at the top of a hill right in my path. Not only did this take place in an instant, but the individual wearing Rollerblades never offered so much as a yoo-hoo to announce his presence.

Rollerblades might be against the law in Oklahoma. I know nothing about them or the folks who wear them. Nor do I know who or what was attached to that pair. I do know that when I made my exit, Madam did not accompany me. Instead, she took an unexpected route out of the saddle and over my head, followed by a three-point landing in the tall grass. In an attempt to avoid a serious fender-bender, I leaped over her, clearing the most important body parts but clanking her helmet a good one with my shoe.

I then covered a generous piece of ground in the following seconds. It's safe to say I made a faster trip to the nearest hilltop than I ever made out of a starting gate. Only then did I remember that Madam had taken a different course of action. The rollerblader now stood gawking at her landing site. No movement there.

"Lady, are you okay?" he called cautiously. Nothing stirred in the tall grass. He called again, "Can I help you?" Then he looked toward me, somewhat accusingly.

Me oh my, now what should I do? We'd started out this day in perfect harmony. How did we arrive at such a rude separation? Oh, how I wanted to get my hooves on those nasty little wheels that guy had strapped to his feet! Meanwhile, Madam and I faced a pivotal moment in our budding friendship. It was time to take a deep breath and think fast, if I wanted to save it.

You might imagine my relief when Madam struggled to her feet, dusted off, and slowly took full account of the scene. Her eyes slipped past the alien, drifted beyond the biking path, breezed over a distant picnic table, and came to rest on me. The look on her face made the alien seem downright friendly! Oh boy, maybe she would forgive me if I hustled back, made my sincere apologies, and delivered her home, more or less intact. It seemed worth a try. Nonetheless, she looked menacing. Maybe she was in a state of shock.

My trip back down the hill matched the one going up—fast. The alien had obviously never met a galloping horse, and I confess to smiling at his terror. A man wearing wheels on his feet does not constitute a common sight, especially with his mouth agape and his wheels frozen to the path. Of course, I had no intention of running over him, though giving him a good scare seemed reasonable. Next time, maybe he'd remember a little trail courtesy. In fact, I thought I might contact the Three Rivers Parks Association and demand some new road signs, but it was time to pay attention to the problem at hand.

It was when Madam called to the alien, suggesting he catch my bridle reins as I passed him, that he regained consciousness.

"What?" he squeaked.

"He's very gentle," she warbled back to him.

"Yes, I can see that!" he replied in obvious disbelief.

He did *not* reach for my reins. Meanwhile, I reached Madam, just as she gingerly made her way to a picnic table, where she sat and coolly assessed the damage. She looked a mess, with grass-stained breeches, her new Troxel helmet cock-eyed on her head, and the unbecoming blemish on her nose. Dear me, this looked bad. No doubt the nose wound had something to do with my hoof clipping her helmet as I exited the crash scene.

Lack of experience with this kind of catastrophe left me speechless. I took a chance and gave Madam a friendly nudge on the shoulder that displayed the least amount of grass stain. No response. This peace offering didn't spark any foul language from her, though, so I gave it another try. She finally looked me in the eye and sighed.

"Noah, where was all that speed when you needed to win a futurity race?"

Now, I might have been new at this relationship business, but I was no dummy. This was *not* the time or place to remind her that it was the starting gate and the trainer that brought an end to my racing career, not my lack of speed. That discussion would have to wait for another day.

Without another word, the alien pushed off and sped over the hill, with sparks flying from his wheels. It looked as if he'd sustained no injuries from his encounter with me, though I would not guarantee he was wearing clean shorts when we parted company.

And now I had to figure out how to get Madam off that picnic table and back into the saddle. She resisted my anxious nudging and took her sweet time inspecting body parts, including her nose. Mind you, she did not inspect me for lumps or bruises.

Finally, between the two of us, we managed to get her back on board and sitting more or less upright. It was a long and quiet walk back to Evergreen. While I dithered about where my next home might be, she must have been worrying about her over-extended neck. It suddenly felt like my place in the household could be at risk. I kept trying to picture life as a school horse at Camp Manitou or as a research project at the University of California–Davis. Neither sounded so great.

Though all this worry left me headachy, luck prevailed once again. Our ill-fated trail ride in Baker Park came to a surprisingly decent end. After offering my most sincere apologies for depositing her in the shrubs, Madam patted me encouragingly for my effort.

"We'll try it again," she offered rather weakly, "once I can hold my head up straight and recover from my black eye."

I then noticed that Omar's partner, Monica, was sitting in her car, waiting for Madam. The two of them drove away from Evergreen, though not in the direction of St. Paul. Later, I heard the landlords say the two drove to McCafferty's Pub for some kind of therapy. Well, that seemed like a good idea. Maybe McCafferty's Pub offered chiropractic services.

8

Meeting Ghillie

Ghillie: a Scottish or Irish fishing guide

Nobody told me that Madam's extended family included another horse—or even another pet. For all I know, she has a large collection of pets vying for her affection. Or perhaps she's a horse hoarder. After that morning's eye-opener, I would not have been surprised to find that she was stashing horses and other beasties in her garage. Lucky me—I was the guy who got to discover these hidden treasures. Not that I'm jealous, mind you. It just made me wonder how much undisclosed information was out there, waiting to surface at some inopportune moment.

First, I accidently met her Fluff Muffin Cat in Evergreen's lunchroom. This was the one with a tendency toward hypochondria. Then came the elderly Jack Russell, her constant travel companion, who rode shotgun on the console of Madam's Subaru Outback. And let me not forget my suspicions about Madam's trips to Wisconsin and Oklahoma. I'm convinced these outings will eventually turn up details about more pets and clandestine doings. Today, my discovery turned out to be another horse. Tomorrow, it could be a litter of potbelly pigs wanting to share my room. It's a worry.

I might not have discovered him at all if that saucy pony Gilbert hadn't brought my attention to a frail-looking thoroughbred gelding in the end paddock. According to Gilbert, the guy in question belonged to Madam. Gadzooks! Another surprise! There he stood, pale as a sculpture in Madame Tussauds Wax Museum. Still as a stone, head hung low, and leaning against a linden tree for support, he did not look like a rock star. What he looked like was a guy in need of a lot of groceries and an extended vacation. Gilbert also reported the shaky stranger had an unusual name—Ghillie. According to Gilbert, who operated high on Evergreen's information chain, Ghillie meant guide. To be more precise, it meant an Irish fishing guide.

Having never traveled to Ireland, I can only say that Evergreen Farm offers limited fly-fishing, and the horse we were looking at certainly had no plans to guide anglers. To the contrary, he looked as if he could use some guidance from a good veterinarian.

Once I recovered from the shock of eyeballing a new sibling, I decided to ease myself next door, and learn more about him. This required operating a tricky gate, but I was getting good at this gate business. I managed to free myself and slip over for a little meeting with Ghillie. He did not, however, offer a grand reception. He barely lifted his head to acknowledge my arrival.

Mr. Ghillie looked even worse close up—disturbingly worse. Though he wore a flysheet that covered his major body parts, I could see his bony shoulders and hips poking through the thin fabric. His angular shape gave him the appearance of a tall coat rack. His hair coat and mane didn't look so great either. I made a note to myself to offer him some of my new silk shampoo and hair conditioner. Maybe Madam could give him a good spa treatment to shine him up.

It was hard to tell if he saw me as I moved closer to his paddock. With his eyes half closed, he took long, slow breaths, followed by uneven sighs. Hmm ... maybe he was meditating. A small, untouched pile of hay lay on the ground next to a water bucket. Though I usually enjoy chatting up strangers, this one presented a communication challenge. How did one horse speak to another when the listener appeared to be in a coma? A good barn joke hardly seemed like a place to begin. I thought of asking him to take a stroll, but poor old Ghillie didn't look ready for strolling. Besides, the landlord would hear about it. She also would question my opening gates and inviting myself in to meet new neighbors.

"Ahem," I finally offered, giving myself enough space to make an escape if need be. "A decent afternoon, don't you think?"

Much to my surprise, Ghillie spoke right up. "Ahem yourself," he replied. "Yes, a lovely day. Tell me how you managed to open my gate."

Good grief! A courteous, though rather commanding voice, I thought. "Well, it's something new I've been practicing," I answered. "A draft horse friend gave me some tips."

Then Ghillie asked my name and where I lived. How long had I been at Evergreen? What did I do for a living? Did I have a girlfriend? On and on he went, rattling off a list of questions that, quite frankly, took me aback. Our little meet-and-greet was beginning to feel like a *60 Minutes* interview.

"Well … err … let's see," I said. "I'm new here. Nearly became a futurity racehorse. That didn't work out. Looking for a new career. Wouldn't mind managing a few cattle. Not crazy about dressage. Maybe a writer." Oh boy, that sounded pretty lame. "Ah, well, I guess I don't really have a horse job, at least not yet," I continued, my mouth firing off thoughts like hail on a tin roof. "Or is it a profession I'm looking for?" I wondered out loud. "Yes, a writing career—that's it. And I like to play cards." Oh, dear. I had no idea what I was talking about.

Maybe this guy wasn't sick at all. Maybe he was an interrogator for the FBI. Who said I needed a profession anyway? I already was planning to win the Pulitzer Prize for half-fiction. And by the way, for such a weak-looking pup, this Mr. Ghillie conducted a probing interview! It was hard to look away from him, though. He seemed to know things about me that I had not yet told him. Maybe this was what they meant by a "horse whisperer," a horse that kept track of classified information.

After all, we'd barely said hello before he launched himself right into my personal affairs. He must have noticed my growing unease because he changed the subject.

"I suppose you wonder why I look like this," he offered, noting my frown. "Yes, I know I'm thin and pathetic-looking. That's why Madam gave me a nice flysheet to wear, so people would stop whispering gossip and asking what happened to me. Actually, I'm looking much better than I did a month ago." Then he dropped the bomb. "Like you, I also came from Oklahoma, last October to be exact."

Like me? What the heck? How does he know I came from Oklahoma? Something's fishy here, I thought.

"Then, just about the time I settled into this place, my kidneys stopped working—Lyme disease," said Ghillie, ignoring my confused expression. "After that, everything went dark for a few months. I spent three weeks at the university's large animal clinic and many more weeks lying in my room. I only recently started coming outside for a bit of sunshine. Madam has been taking care of me all this time."

Well, that explained a lot. No wonder Madam charged out here every morning at daybreak. All this time I'd thought she was excited to see me or just enjoyed having early coffee with her friends. It also explained why her tack trunk was such a mess. It was stuffed with Ace bandages, syringes, and medications of every description. None of that stuff belonged to me. What's more, this Ghillie kept asking complicated questions, like what I wanted from life. Well, for Pete's sake, his little cross-examination was causing me to hyperventilate. I must say, though, he was polite enough and seemed to mean well.

"Uh, what did you do for a living before you got sick?" I finally asked in an attempt to change the subject.

"Never had much chance to learn a trade," he explained. "Since I can't do much these days, I've decided to just spend my time observing and listening to others. Maybe like you, I also can write about what I learn."

"Observe and listen to what?" I shot back a bit too sharply.

"You mean you just watch the world go by? Don't you plan on getting well someday?" Then it occurred to me that he might not be planning on getting well. Maybe that was all he could do, that and count sheep in the shade of a linden tree.

"Oh, I listen for things, like how people talk to one another and to their horses. Then, I keep track of how they treat their friends and whether they like their jobs. Are they doing what they're meant to do with their lives or becoming what they're meant to be? Are they living the life that wants to live in them? You know, important stuff," he added.

Me oh my, that explained his strange questions. Maybe those deep, philosophical thoughts overtook horses when they got really sick or really old.

"Of course I'm living the life that wants to live in me! What an odd question," I declared. "I'm just having a little trouble sorting out what that life might be. This place is full of overachievers, you know. It's just that I'm more interested in achieving at gin rummy and hoofleball than at a half-pass or a pirouette, if you get my drift. Dressage is not exactly living in me."

Surely he couldn't believe this was a character flaw. It was not my fault that everything looked like a possibility. "I just happen to say yes to new ideas more often than most horses do. How bad can that be?" I asked him.

"Not bad at all," said Ghillie with a wry smile.

Holy cow, he can read my thoughts! I just know it.

With that, Ghillie closed his eyes and dropped off to dreamsville without so much as a cheerio. It looked like our chat had come to an end, at least for the moment.

9

Too Many Choices

Now that I'd nailed down my writing career, and Madam and I were an official partnership, I saw a new dilemma looming on the horizon. Let's just say my introduction and curious interview with Mr. Ghillie sparked an identity crisis of sorts—for me, that is. I thought I knew who I was, but now I can see life presented too many choices. Whether it was shopping for horse cookies at the Waconia Co-Op or exploring career options in the Cutting Horse Chatter (the last word in the cutting horse business), even a smart fellow can get flummoxed trying to make heavy-duty life decisions. Plus, I did not know any equine guidance counselors, so I was hanging out on my own in a strange land, trying to figure things out.

Back in the day, a talented guy such as I could have counted on a career without a jumble of choices. I'm called an Appendix quarter horse, a specialty breed that traditionally looked for employment that required speed. This, of course, was how I landed on a racetrack with a trainer who also could have used a guidance counselor. Incidentally, several of my cousins excelled in barrel racing, another honorable speed profession for Appendix quarter horses. Anyhoo, I got my pink slip from the Oklahoma racing department and bingo—suddenly I found myself up north in Norwegian territory, trying to write a book and figure out what to do with the rest of my life. It also came to my attention that career choices abounded here in the Midwest, though most of the hot ones seemed to be in health care. Too bad Madam could not afford to send me to medical school, though I wasn't the least bit interested in becoming a medical research subject like Ned. So that took care of that idea.

Problem number one, as I saw it, was that this writing life gave me a bigger view of the world and all the previously undiscovered choices. A case in point: I recently had a new vocational flash when Omar and I dropped in at the Scott County Draft Horse Exposition. We sat for hours watching the Belgian horse competition. Then came the Percheron teams, followed by the Shires. Let me tell you, those boys cut an imposing swath with their buff physiques and lavish harnesses. They maneuvered great rumbling wagons around the arena without so much as running down an announcer. And wow, the female members of those outfits stepped right up as the official team captains. And we were mighty impressed with their grand sense of style—equine chic at its best. My, my, that display sent me directly into a new career reverie. Perhaps a bejeweled harness and red driving cart were in my future.

Another case in point: the next week, Madam and I headed out, with Spruce and me in the Comfy Sundowner trailer. We spent the day taking in one more mind-boggling horse performance—a National Reining Horse Association futurity. This cool western riding event involved athletic ability and willingness of a horse to perform patterns, plus spins and sliding stops. Wow! While I was long on athletic ability, the willingness part gave me pause. Sticking to instructions and patterns might be a stretch, though I could handle those sliding stops with panache. That, plus I had the excellent hair going for me, a must with the reining crowd. Honestly, the reining futurity really did pique my interest, but my new Evergreen pals tended to stick their noses in the air when it came to cowboy sports. So I took at least a temporary pass on reining.

I'd almost forgotten this obsessive hankering of mine to cut cattle. Now this struck me as a natural choice for a quarter horse, though Spruce said I'm a bit tall for the job. And another thing, the only cattle near Evergreen Farm grazed indifferently across the road from us. Other than a quick sprint around the pasture when mosquito control helicopters flew over, those cows hardly moved. They certainly showed no interest in cutting or even in exchanging pleasantries, for that matter.

So all these choices came to light once again when I decided to try jumping. It started with a lesson from Louise. This turned out to be great fun; plus, it required no big investments in carriages or fancy harnesses. Now, jumping is my favorite thing. Jumping most any obstacle appealed to me, except maybe a Rollerblader. Beyond that I could appreciate jumping anything from a triple oxer to a Buick. What's more, Madam liked jumping too. Even when I miscalculated distance or height, she'd shout, "Yahoo!" like a ten-year-old at a Roy Rogers movie. Could this be another life path or employment alternative? Of course it could. Then, Madam gently reminded me of the Scott County Draft Horse Exposition and my brief pout when she refused to purchase a thousand-dollar red driving cart.

"Let's just have fun jumping," she exclaimed. "You don't have to make it your life's work."

Well, I'd arrived at an identity crossroads. Madam and I discussed this at length. She suggested I might want to simplify my life and stop worrying about new careers, at least until we finished our first book. So for now, I was determined to streamline things. I'd just stick to a bit of cribbage, my weekly Spanish lessons, baking from my new King Arthur baking bible, singing in Evergreen's glee club, and managing my Facebook fan page. That should help clean up the schedule.

10

The Art of Training Humans

It takes a long time to train a human. None of this "get them broke in thirty days and into competition by age two" philosophy works with two-legged partners. It takes time and creativity on a horse's part to get past all those self-assured human ways. In fact, most humans don't know the difference between a horse problem and a horse lesson. Typically, they think training setbacks begin and end with the horse, though I beg to differ. I once heard a fellow blame his horse's poor performance on the fact that the horse grew faster on one end than on the other. Now, this revelation caused quite a hoot in the horse community. We never did figure out which end grew faster, the rump or the withers. The gelding looked pretty even on both ends.

Then, there was the self-proclaimed cowboy who thought the answer to every training mishap was to strap on a set of hobbles—those annoying ankle bracelets that prevent a horse from freelance touring around the neighborhood. Yes, I know the uncomfortable restraints might encourage a horse to stick around home, rather than hang out in the Johnson's garden, but a little food bribery can achieve the same results. For reasons that escape me, humans like to hobble any moving creature that shows signs of unbridled enthusiasm. (Forgive the pun.)

Horse trainers come in a variety of flavors, ranging from horse "dudes" to genuine horsemen and horsewomen. Horse dudes talk a lot about their talent. Horsemen talk less and appear to live their talent. Horse dudes apply bungee cords and other Rube Goldberg training gimmicks. Horsemen watch and listen. Horse dudes think they know everything they need to know and don't bother watching or listening. Horsemen see each day as an occasion to learn something new about us. They also know how to play with their horse partners, a talent we horses sincerely appreciate, by the way.

Of course, horses know all this because we do a lot of observing and listening and very little talking, except among ourselves. Never mind that I occasionally squeal during certain training exercises. The truth is that most horses start out life with few unpleasant thoughts or habits. I have noticed, however, that some horse dudes are good at transforming perfectly sensible horses into renegades. This looks like a lot of hard work to me, but horse dudes don't seem to mind. Or maybe they just don't recognize their own achievements.

As for me, I've always felt it was more important to be interested in the world than to be an interesting training prospect, although not every horse trainer would agree with this philosophy. In fact, this might explain why I was in Minnesota learning how to pirouette, instead of living the futurity high life. While I might not have been wild about Madam's dressage program, it was delightful to see the world via my Comfy Sundowner trailer. While our training might inhibit the natural flow of daily life, the Comfy Sundowner opened the door to all kinds of discoveries and entertainment.

Take natural horsemanship, sometimes called horse whispering. This trend was booming, which confirmed my theory that too many people used unnatural approaches to training. I know that natural horsemanship was supposed to promote submission by using gentle methods. Who could argue with that? It also aimed to develop a calmer, happier, and more willing horse partner—another splendid goal. But the idea that it appealed to our instincts made me chuckle. My instincts must fall outside natural; convincing me to conform would require a course in miracles. On the other hand, an arrowroot biscuit or McDonald's French fry could help move the training ball along nicely.

Finally, consider the concept of teaching a horse to partner with people. Well, hello! Some of us know perfectly well how to work and play with people. We just prefer achieving this through civil discourse than jury-rigged bungee cords wound around our butts.

Madam, as it turned out, viewed natural horsemanship with an appreciative eye. Hence, our drills began with some on-the-ground exercises to help me pay attention. I liked this, except for the routine called flagging. This involved first an old pillowcase and later a plastic bag tied to a stick. Madam rubbed the pillowcase over my body, a move that seemed harmless enough. However, I had a change of heart when she got to the plastic bag-waving maneuver. No doubt she intended to ease my fears of strange, flapping objects. Unfortunately, I'm still opposed to strange flapping objects.

Next, Madam presented me with the bridle. Frankly, cold, hard bits between my teeth have never held much appeal. In fact, Madam would say that teaching me the basics of bridling stretched her patience just a tad. It also stretched my imagination and gave me my first human training opportunity.

I might not have mentioned how much I dislike tight clothes. This includes summer outerwear worn for fly protection—way too body-hugging! It also includes stiff girths, snug shipping boots, tight nosebands, and anything else that restricts freedom and inspiration, even a bridle. This brings me to a recent incident involving both the bridle and my tongue. I'm not sure how it happened, but my tongue suddenly grew too big for my mouth. It could have been a bee sting or a frond from some timothy hay, though one would think I'd have noticed that. Even the vet declared she had no idea what caused such an unpleasant development. Whatever the cause, my fat tongue was none too becoming, especially when I started to drool.

On the other hand, this tongue-tying nonsense laid the groundwork for lots of comforting hot packs on my chin. Madam and the landlord took care to see that I enjoyed the cool breeze of not one but two fans refreshing my room. After a day or two, Madam decided it was time for me to get out for some exercise. That was when I seized the opportunity to do some training of my own. When it came time for her to buckle the bridle noseband, I signaled that this caused me discomfort. I yawned widely and sighed. I even coughed and twitched to indicate pain at the touch of the confounded noseband. Off it went. The next challenge involved the bit. This, of course, presented another chance for me to shape out a collaborative training program. After I made it clear that a bit was out of the question, Madam went to work reassembling the bridle. When she finished, it looked more like a dog leash than a steering device. It felt perfectly comfortable too. (Actually, it still feels comfortable today, as she brings it out of the tack trunk from time to time.) Of course, Madam believed the whole thing was her idea.

My training success didn't end there. I used the same approach to get rid of the bridle altogether. After a little groaning on my part, Madam suggested we ditch the bridle and ride with a halter. No bridle, no problem.

After a little fine-tuning, I operated quite well wearing nothing on my head except a fashionably long forelock. We even took a few jumps this way when the spirit moved us. Yet this exercise prompted some bad choices on the part of others at Evergreen Farm—like the day I awoke to a woman screaming, "Whoa!" as her big gelding Bruce galloped full speed past my window. He wore nothing but his rider. That's when the landlords put their foot down about untested training equipment—or lack thereof. Of course, I'm back in a bridle.

11

Bedlam in Buffalo County

Sometimes I wonder about Madam's past. Most days she seems levelheaded, but a little observation on my part tells me she could be some kind of closet cowgirl. She didn't always behave quite as primly or properly as one might think. Hints of this appeared every now and again when she cruised through the barn in a pair of Rio of Mercedes western boots. Then sometimes she buckled into a pair of handmade chaps for one of our little trail rides. These chaps, by the by, saw a lot more saddle time than a few spins around Baker Park. Honestly, most places we ride don't require any leg protection. Besides, western chaps don't mix so well with dressage wear, though that never bothered Madam. In any case, these little disconnects caused me to wonder whether she might be living a double life—in fact, I knew she was living a double life. Hadn't I recently met the other horse in her life, stashed in a paddock right under my nose?

Another thing about Madam's travel habits—she regularly packed a large duffle and left town for a week or so without me. Since most business trips require a proper suitcase, not a large duffle, I suspected her journeys did *not* include work. I was convinced these secret getaways involved other horses and maybe even cattle. As a self-respecting American quarter horse who could use a little cattle action, this disappearing act of hers frustrated me. Why would she leave me home to mince around an arena with my mane braided up like Pippi Longstocking? It just made better sense to be sorting Herefords.

I finally asked her where she went that required parking me with all the hothouse dressage flowers. Her answer surprised me. It so happened she'd been visiting her ranching friends, all the way from Wisconsin to Oklahoma and even to Montana. Imagine not breathing a word of this to me! She also admitted that the Wisconsin delegation kept her busy working on weekends. Imagine that—more surprises. This woman really *was* living a secret cowgirl life. Well, I put my hoof down and insisted that any future sojourns to Wisconsin and elsewhere would include me. Amazingly, Madam agreed. Maybe she was just waiting until we got to know one another better before we jumped into a travel arrangement. Anyway, from that day forward, every trip across the St. Croix River to western Wisconsin produced monumental mayhem. Admittedly, a few incidents caused my hair to stand on end, but I also learned through trial and (mostly) error to either get smart at ranch work or stay out of the way. The trick is to know which course to choose.

Madam's Wisconsin friends, the McGarrys, owned a big piece of land that was once a family dairy farm. They grew corn, hay, and assorted livestock. This was no ordinary ranch, for two reasons. First, it ran by an unusual set of business principles that would confuse most accountants. Second—and I'm mildly surprised by this—the place had not come to the attention of the Bureau of Alcohol, Tobacco, Firearms, and Explosives.

Not that a lot of shooting took place at the McGarrys', but there were occasions when gunfire and squealing tires sparked up the night. Plus, one neighbor, Rodney Heimlich, periodically scaled the McGarrys' roof at 1:00 a.m. to serenade the family. None of the McGarrys appreciated Rodney's crooning.

What's more, the entertainment went beyond midnight warbling. Morning light often revealed a curious mix of farm-friendly items deposited in the yard. These did not arrive by UPS. One day it might be a new half-ton pickup truck. The next day could feature a dozen Powder River pasture gates or a set of John Deere tractor tires. In fact, McGarrys' property looked more like a farm auction site than a peaceful little cattle spread. One morning, we found two coon-hunting mules tied to a stock trailer, enjoying a bale of hay. (I'll get back to this topic later.) Few details accompanied these mysterious deliveries. I could only assume they involved one of the McGarry business ventures. Nobody ever asked or explained which one.

Jack McGarry made an obvious living raising American quarter horses and a few hundred head of beef cattle. He made a less apparent living buying, selling, and trading just about anything— draft horses, fencing materials, bits, Redbone hounds, miscellaneous farm machinery, anonymous steers, cavalry memorabilia, and World War II artillery. Occasionally, Jack also loaned items that belonged to others. Such was the case with a custom-built saddle that once belonged to Madam. Jack generously offered it to a veterinarian friend to take to Wyoming, elk hunting. I now know why Madam no longer owns a western stock saddle. It seems Jack's elk-hunter friend lost both the saddle and his horse to thieves. Consequently, all this buying and trading made for a unique business that occasionally triggered the interest of local law enforcement. Jack was an entrepreneur for challenging economic times.

On my first visit to McGarrys', I could see that Jack delegated most of the ranch work to his wife, Marcie. Madam helped pick up the slack. No wonder she kept disappearing on weekends. I saw that these two women spent hours sorting and doctoring livestock. Jack, for his part, kept the fires of commerce burning, while Marcie, Madam, and any drop-in neighbors rounded up brood mares, patched fences, and tackled calves that needed vaccinating. On day one of our first visit, Jack blissfully drove his Belgian pulling horse team around the hayfield, while the rest of his crew chased some steers that had made a run for an open gate. Actually, Jack forgot to close the gate after driving his team through. As a newcomer to this Wisconsin style of cowboying, I kept a sharp eye on everything. Nothing was more embarrassing than stepping crosswise in a gopher hole or locking oneself in a pen or getting run down by a cranky mother cow. Madam, didn't seem too concerned about anything, so I decided to go by her agenda, not mine.

The first day passed with only minor mishaps. By day two, Jack had become bored with his pulling horse training. He saddled up a ranch horse named Marvin and joined us, much to Marcie and Madam's chagrin. Marvin seemed to understand his job, though I could see right away that Jack excelled in directing the action, rather than supporting it. The morning's tasks began with separating some mother cows from their calves. I stayed out of the way as best I could, for fear of getting a bullwhip cracked over my backside. Meanwhile, the peaceful morning soon erupted in a jumble of shouting. Barking dogs and a liberal dose of colorful language followed. Calves bolted, gates swung on their hinges, mother cows bawled, and every horse scrambled for cover. The dust was so thick, I couldn't see what got caught and what got away.

After a few threats of divorce, things finally settled down and everyone retreated to a safe spot. It was then we realized a John Deere dealer, who had stopped in to talk business with Jack, unwisely joined the fracas and accidently got vaccinated for blackleg. Since Marcie was the only one holding a syringe, we figured she must have been the author of that little misstep. The John Deere guy might have escaped death from blackleg, but he wasted no time getting into his pickup and out the driveway. He claimed he would come back later in the week, when the ranch work was done. He could see that McGarrys were setting up for a branding, and my guess is he had a long list of safer jobs to get done.

Beyond the McGarry ranch doings, Buffalo County also is home to an impressive number of saloons—make that, an impressive number of disorderly saloons. Before calling it a day, Marvin and I found ourselves saddled and ready for action, yet standing in the stock trailer in front of the Dim View Saloon. While our crew enjoyed some liquid refreshment indoors, we took in the action outside, including a brief thunderstorm storm and lightning strike that knocked out the Dim View's power. Darkness combined with free-flowing adult beverages set the stage for a chair-pitching tournament. This turned into a bet that someone couldn't break down the ladies restroom door. In due course, the restroom door came down, accompanied by screams from inside the stalls. The brawl quickly moved outside to the parking lot. This gave everyone more room for self-expression. Marvin and I also enjoyed a better view once the entertainment fired up outside.

About this time, we noticed a cowboy relaxing in a lawn chair in the bed of his pickup. The guy started cheering for his brother-in-law, who was taking quite a thumping from a biker. Several customers then turned on their headlights to better illuminate the scuffle. Meanwhile, Jack, who was still inside the Dim View, got into a heated debate with a neighbor over a horse deal. Apparently, the deal worked out better for Jack than for the neighbor. Unable to resolve their quarrel, Jack marched out to his stock trailer, where I tried my best to crouch behind Marvin. Thankfully, Jack was not looking for me but unloaded Marvin and picked up a lariat. Much to my astonishment—and probably Marvin's—Jack stepped into the saddle and rode Marvin into the Dim View. By the way, Jack throws a rope better than most. Hence, he proceeded to rope the peeved neighbor and haul him a few revolutions around the bar. I learned later that this prank caused quite a response from the bartender, who also served as the bouncer. He immediately started tossing miscellaneous farmers out of his saloon. This created a flurry of lime green and lavender bridesmaid dresses, as a wedding party scrambled for the back door of the Dim View. The group scrambled through the parking lot and ran on down the road, leaving their vehicle behind. As for me, I wondered where in the world Madam had gone and how she'd gotten mixed up with this collection of characters.

We soon learned that Madam and Marcie had returned to the ranch to start dinner. Therefore, they missed most of the uproar—a good thing. Someone must have called Marcie to report Jack's roping performance, because she showed up just about the time the fight broke up. Amused would not have described the look on her face as she loaded Marvin in the trailer and took us home. Fortunately, everyone else made it back safely from the Dim View. Only one unclaimed pickup remained in McGarrys' driveway the next morning. According to Madam, everyone sat around the breakfast table, drinking their coffee without a word. I assumed things would be pretty quiet after the previous evening's performance, but no. Marcie had a few things to say about the Dim View hubbub. Plus that, she had a long list of chores she expected to see completed before noon.

Well, you might imagine my shock when Marvin announced we would be going coon hunting that evening—*all* of us, meaning Madam, the McGarrys, a couple of bluetick coonhounds named Jeb and Bob, and two Missouri mules named Charlie and Harry. The mules looked too small to be of use to anybody, but according to Marvin, they understood the finer points of coon hunting better than the rest of the group, including the hounds. By this time, I felt confident that Marvin held the most accurate information of anyone present.

Someone made a decision that the McGarrys' son Jackson would bring Marvin and me along, in case anybody got tired of walking. As a card-carrying pacifist, I'm not fond of guns or hunting, so this plan didn't much appeal to me. Consequently, I began planning my own strategy to avoid getting shot, bitten, or kicked. It never occurred to me that these hunters rarely loaded their guns. When they did, it involved shooting a soup can off fence posts. I also noticed the hounds preferred chasing everything except coons. The two spent most the evening tracking chipmunks and woodchucks. As for the mules, they preferred to avoid overextending themselves. It looked like I might be in luck. Since coon hunting officially started later in the evening, maybe we would just go for a little nighttime stroll in the woods and knock off a few soup cans. When the hour arrived, off we went into the darkness.

"What makes a good coonhound?" I heard Madam ask Jack as we paraded up the hills and along the tree line.

"Natural ability and training," Jack explained seriously. I could see little evidence of either. "The best teacher is an experienced hound," he continued. Jack must have been referring to the older bluetick named

Jeb. We spotted him cantering across the field in the direction of home. "A young dog must be closely supervised," Jack rambled on. "Allowing it to roam loose at night is an invitation to trouble."

With one loose hound heading for home, and the other in pursuit of the neighbor's Scottish highland bull, I wondered about Jack's coonhound training program.

The mules, on the other hand, understood the plan better than the hounds. Madam rode Charlie, who scaled the steep hillsides and plowed through the underbrush with ease. Each time they came to a wire fence, she laid a jacket over the wire, and the mule hopped over like rabbit. These mules didn't even shy when we discovered Monte Labowski, one of last night's Dim View agitators, napping in the middle of the lane. Fortunately, he was not in possession of any firearms.

The fearless hunters wore miner's lamps on their heads, enabling them to locate anything worth tracking. We simply walked along behind the parade, while Jack continued his lecture on training and hunting hounds. Since Madam and I knew precious little about hounds, Jack took the opportunity to educate us on their voices. For instance, we learned that hound voices come in three flavors. An open trailer begins to bark as soon as it hits the track and continues barking all the way to the tree. Well, it appeared we had one of those. He woke up the night as we processed through the woods like a circus train.

Jack continued, unaffected by the rioting hound. "A semi-silent hound barks at the track but remains silent until it gets to the tree," he explained, again serious. "The third, the silent hound, hunts soundlessly until actually treeing a coon."

We seemed to have one open trailer. As the second hound disappeared without so much as a whisper minutes after exiting his kennel, he must have been the silent type. Beyond the voice issue, I wasn't sure Jeb and Bob offered the best examples of coon-hunting style. We eventually found the two of them savoring a moldy deer leg on McGarrys' back step. Buffalo County raccoons must still be talking about that impressive hunting exhibition. Nevertheless, I appreciated the lack of gunfire, and the mules added a nice touch. Day two passed, with Buffalo County's woodland creatures safely out of harm's way.

The following morning, Madam rushed out early to visit with me. She suggested we get ourselves packed up and on the road for home right after breakfast. This sounded like an excellent choice. So I bid adieu to Marvin and strolled outside to wait for her next to the Comfy Sundowner. While Madam finished her coffee and said her good-byes to Marcie, Jack popped out the kitchen door to intercept a visitor coming up the driveway in a rusted-out farm truck. Thankfully, he intercepted the visitor, as it looked like the guy was heading my way.

"Mornin'," called Jack to the fellow behind the wheel. "Mornin' yourself," barked a fearsome-looking guy dressed in greasy bib overalls and no shirt. With arms the size of tree trunks, decorated with an array of tattoos, he made a stunning picture. Jack, however, must have smelled a piece of business coming his way, because he showed no signs of alarm at the driver's appearance

"Tell me about that horse," said the visitor, pointing my way.

"What do you want to know?" retorted Jack.

"Is he for sale?" the guy queried.

"Everything around here is for sale at the right price," rejoined Jack.

Oh boy, this does not sound right at all, I thought. Where in the world was Madam when I needed her? She was lingering over coffee and doughnuts when she should have been out here telling Mr. Big Bibs to take a powder. We need to leave this instant!

"I'm a hunter," roared Big Bibs. "Kin a fella shoot a gun off him?"

Jack paused and thought about the question for a few seconds. "A fella can do anything off him once," he finally answered, planting a smart slap on my backside.

Yikes, I'd rather go for grand prix dressage than take a ride out west, elk hunting with Big Bibs. I had half a mind to give old Jack a swift boot in his behind. No need for that, though. Madam watched from the kitchen as this little performance unfolded. Out the door she trotted, duffel bag in hand.

"Good morning, boys," she offered in her most cheerful morning voice. "We were just about to load up." She nodded to me and firmly pointed at the open trailer door. No need to point twice. I leaped in, and she locked up the tailgate. She wasted no time settling behind the big Ram's steering wheel.

"Well, at least he loads good," laughed Mr. Big Bibs.

Jack just waved us off, shouting that he would be looking for our help again in a few weeks.

12

The Writing Life

Our visit to McGarrys' gave me a whole new appreciation for Evergreen Farm and my safe little room. Omar greeted me with a deck of cards and a cribbage board, and even Ghillie inquired with great interest about the midnight coon-hunting caper.

"What a relief it was to say good-bye to Mr. Big Bibs," I told him. "And furthermore, coon hunting will not be showing up on my list of possible careers!"

Fortunately, the only hunting that went on around here involved Snuggles pursuing a few pocket gophers. No guns, no delinquent hounds, only great appreciation to be back with my friends in my home-sweet-home.

I decided to take advantage of some down time to appraise my budding writing career, beginning with my new logo, created by our brilliant designer friend Ms. Nancy. She quizzed me at length before putting pen to paper, and I think she captured the essence of my personality—or my "brand," as the marketing people like to say. "An equine original!" (Her words, not mine.) Once it was finished, we had to find a clever way to apply this masterpiece to something besides my homepage. It deserved more than a single public appearance. I thought perhaps a small video production was in order—the movie business always held a certain appeal.

The charming graphic design also lent itself to embroidering on a stylish clothing item. Well, what could a horse do but jump on Google to search for the perfect fashion accessory on which to showcase the logo? As much as I appreciate a good hat, those logo-laden ball caps seem rather passé. Then there's the coffee mug or the T-shirt worn by every Tom, Dick, and Larry, but we don't need to fill up our closets with more bric-a-brac. What this really called for was a blast of color, style, and panache!

This is where Madam came into the picture. Her personal style trends toward mix-and-more-or-less match (often short on the "match" part). Yet some days she knocks it right out of the barn. This usually happens when she dons one of those fetching silk scarves she adores. Madam must own a dozen of them, and I have to admit, they brighten up a dull ensemble. Ms. Nancy and I already were working on the final product design and applying it to the lovely scarves, or "wild rags," as a friend called them. Now we needed someone who could run one of those fancy sewing machines.

Speaking of style, that bad boy Patrick was not helping my career one bit. Even though he was a guy who hardly noticed fashion, Patrick served as Evergreen's unofficial barber. "Unofficial" meant he had more enthusiasm about barbering than talent. Specifically, he ate a section of my mane and also took quite a chink out of my tail. It wasn't pretty. It also created a serious problem with my smartly turned out author image. After all, I'd invested much of my allowance in designer hair products to enhance the bravura tresses. Why? Because my mane and tail perfectly suited the confident, vaguely mysterious look I was working on. Luxurious hair also made a fine fly whisk—and it happened to work well as a chick magnet.

No doubt about it: this writing life presented a heap of

challenges, from problem hair to image management. It also knocked a dent in my daily play schedule. Writing books, attending to a blog, and posting photos on my Facebook fan page seriously detracted from leisure activities. While I respect a healthy work ethic, all these deadlines and photo shoots took a toll. One week, I played only one measly game of *Words with Friends* all week.

And here's another sticky wicket: writer's block. (That's what Madam called it.) She cautioned me about this occupational hazard the day I decided to write a book, but as an independent guy, capable of solving my own problems, I ignored her warning. She then offered a few details about writer's block. Apparently, anyone can develop this disorder. Sometimes a simple thank-you note or a term paper on monarch butterflies can set it off. Political speechwriters must know a lot about writer's block, given the recurring sound bites that jump out of the barn radio.

According to Madam, writer's block symptoms vary but always bring writing to a screeching halt. She described the malady as an overpowering urge to clean the garage or sort boxes of family photos. Sometimes, she herself suffered from it and felt a strange desire to mow the lawn, or join Ancestry.com, or retire to the bedroom and make clothes for the cat. According to her, these evasive measures typically are followed by a nap. Supper comes next, topped off by a longing to take quick spin through the house with the Hoover upright. Once complete, this leaves just enough time to read *Bon Appétit*, take a bath before tuning in the early evening news, and hit the sack.

I was beginning to see how this editorial breakdown worked— it felt familiar, anyway. For instance, just yesterday Gabe said I was looking a little plump. This might be caused by writer's block. Not only was I gaining weight and wasting time perusing the tack rooms for horse treats, but I was picking up my room every day. Online surfing became an obsession. Goodness, I even listened to the political debates. Talk about evasive behavior. I actually caught myself chatting up Duane the dentist, just to avoid finishing a blog. If that list of avoidance tactics didn't spell writer's block, nothing did.

As for my recovery, Madam suggested I start by making a list of writing responsibilities and checking tasks off as I completed them. For example, she recommended writing an apology note to the landlords for spilling cat litter and making a wholesale mess of the tack room. Another suggestion: write a bio to use for public appearances. These seemed like manageable methods of getting back in the groove. Then it occurred to me that as Ghillie now served as my copy editor, maybe a nice walk around the farm with him would inspire me and put me back in the writing mode. It certainly was worth a try.

13

Girl Troubles

Oh, be still my heart. While Madam and I were dabbling in ranch action and finding our way home from the Dim View debacle, the girl of my dreams moved out! Or at least she moved down the road for the summer months. Faith, the heavenly lass with the luminous brown eyes and winning style, was gone. I was delighted to learn, however, that she would be back for a visit on the weekend. The landlord said something about a German dressage teacher holding forth at Evergreen, and dear Faith planned to attend. I might have mentioned that Faith is to dressage what Secretariat is to racing—stunning to watch and impossible to duplicate. (At least, it's impossible for me to duplicate.)

Anyhoo, I'd hardly had a chance to unpack and send my laundry out, and already my thoughts turned to Faith. Such a tailspin she caused for me. Obsessive thinking, Madam called it. Questions flying in every direction made me a little crazy! Had she missed me? Might she stay a while? Me o my, did she have a new boyfriend? Why did she leave? So far, my best courting maneuvers failed to warm her heart much beyond frosty. But I was nothing if not steadfast. Now the question was, should I prepare her room with daisies and fresh oatmeal cookies? Or maybe she would like to watch the movie *Buck*. He was the horse whisperer who knew a thing or two about bonding. It was showing at our outdoor theater in Maple Plain. I hoped that Faith was dreaming sweet dreams of me since Madam and I left for our little foray in Buffalo County.

On the other hand, this "Beat it, Stinky" approach of Faith's would scare a less courageous guy. I had to admit feeling conflicted about her behavior and was beginning to see why the romance business was not meant for the weak or the meek.

Meanwhile, Madam kept suggesting it was time for me to look for a girl who smiled pleasantly at me, rather than from behind clenched teeth. Madam exaggerates, of course, though Faith's smile did sometimes look like she was nursing a toothache. Also, just because Faith occasionally swung her backside in my direction didn't necessarily mean she disliked me. It could be her way of flirting. Oh dear, what was I saying? Perhaps it was time to keep an open mind about meeting someone new. Maybe Gabe could introduce me to his cousin Charlotte from New Jersey. He said she was very sweet and liked to play poker.

My thoughts suddenly were interrupted with another new development. This bit of news also involved bold and independent females. There was yackity, yackity, yak, coming from every room in Evergreen because new neighbors planned to move in soon—and one already had taken up residence in Faith's empty room. He was a nice enough paint fellow named Argo, though he could have taken the next room down the aisle. At least he enjoyed a round of canasta and a good cup of tea. Any newcomers who were serious about card games tended to get along fine around here.

The trouble was that Argo showed up solo, but the landlord expected him to bring a female companion. Word had it that his mysterious lady friend took a pass on traveling with Argo or anyone driving a one-ton pickup truck. In fact, she announced that her plans did not include a five-mile trailer ride, not today, tomorrow or next year. Oh boy, another maid with opinions was headed our way. I was not going to ask this one to go to the movies.

Now this attitude was not so unusual among homebodies who never experienced the thrill of touring the countryside in a Comfy Sundowner trailer. What was rare about her brashness was that the moving episode began three days ago, and she had not yet arrived. For the better part of a week, training experts coaxed, bribed, scolded, and applied every known technique to change this girl's mind. That made the score 3–0 in favor of the mare. She sounded like a cagey woman who might be worth meeting, in case Faith continued to rebuff my advances. (What the heck was the matter with me? I'd just proclaimed that difficult women were officially off my dance card.)

While we all speculated on what day this new gal would arrive, miracle of miracles, a large trailer showed up about lunchtime, just in time for our block party. When the tailgate opened, not one but three imposing damsels stepped out. I don't know where they picked up the other two, but my welcoming speech didn't pique much interest from any of them. They all shot me a glance that shortened my invocation to a quick "hello, nice to meet ya." All three replied to my hospitable greeting with withering gazes, the kind I've come to know so well. Geez, if this kept up, I might need to give up my position as head of Evergreen's welcoming committee.

Two of the newcomers resembled Margaret Thatcher— stern though striking, with an air of political gridlock. The third, the previously mentioned tall, willowy one, wore that "don't fence me in" expression. No need for her to worry, as nobody had any intention of fencing her in. Evergreen Farm seemed to attract a lot of high-maintenance females, both horse and human. Oh well, that just meant we horses needed to work harder on our diplomacy skills.

The Landlord told me the one named Flora had not traveled much. Apparently, she never left her previous home by foot or by trailer. Maybe I could enlighten her about the joys of touring. Or perhaps she would join me for a day trip in the Comfy Sundowner. All these ideas seemed worth consideration. In any case, Flora first had to sober up from the Cosmo cocktails or whatever it was the driver over-served her to get her in the trailer. Once Flora tottered down the ramp and off to her new room, she promptly fell asleep and started to snore.

"Let's let her sleep it off before we plan any welcome receptions," suggested Omar. Good advice.

Now that we were home to three new lasses, plus another visiting princess who arrived on the weekend, Omar and I discussed how to put our best hoof forward. One idea that came to mind was food. I thought about gifts from the kitchen, not the feed mill. Food worked for most situations. Madam certainly knew how to pick up a rolling pin and a basket of apples and turn out a decent pie, which always was a hit. Plus, I'd just signed up for a King Arthur Flour baking class at the Independence Farm and Feed Center. So I brought this foodie idea up with Madam when she stopped in to say good night. She was kind but certainly did not rejoice at my suggestion.

"Dear Noah, you and Omar need to meet some calm girls who appreciate your generosity," she sighed. "I, for one, appreciate you and think we should save your treats from the kitchen for a different kind of a girl. I'm sure you will recognize her when you meet her."

Omar looked dejected. "She might be right," he said. "Baking is hard enough for guys like us. Maybe we can keep the apple pie for our next gin rummy tournament."

14

The Training Disagreement

The management and I stumbled into a small disagreement—
or so she reported to me. She stood at the door, blocking my view of
Doug, a popular farrier who happened to bring his Jack Russell, Gin, to
assist him. Even Madam's elderly Jack Russell enjoyed a visit from Gin.
Hands on her hips, Madam—or in this case, the management— warmed
up with a stern sermon on my departure from our schooling program. Not
that I needed to be reminded of this small detail, but I thought we had an
informal agreement, not an iron-clad contract. I refrained from rolling my
eyes and politely watched Doug pound a few shoes while the
management exercised her lips.

"The experienced dressage rider expects a certain reaction
from her horse in response to light aids," she explained with some
gravity. "Because of his"—this meant me—"mental clarity and high
standards, her horse *supposedly* understands what she wants."

Well, for Pete's sake. She got the mental clarity and high standards right, but who said I didn't understand what she wanted? A light aid is no more than a simple request—a rider courteously asking a horse to do something the horse might or might not feel like doing. I happened to prefer Kool-Aid or lemonade to a light aid. Granted, this could be because I was slightly resistant to Madam's dressage career choice for me. And another thing, every time we took a tour in the Comfy Sundowner, she presented me with a new horse occupation that made dressage seem pretty humdrum. Quite frankly, all this discipline, detail, and personal hygiene stood in the way of genuine fun.

Take the concept of a submissive horse, for example. Compliant, subservient—just what part of this sounds like a good time? It simply did not strike me as compelling goals for horse or human.

And another thing, the management's horse history involved a lot of cow horses, meaning her knowledge of dressage hardly topped mine. Peculiar saddles, cumbersome leg wraps, scratchy bell boots— even dressage "speak" sounded like pig Latin to a horse. Case in point, both the management and I thought a "turn on the haunches" referred to a method of cooking pot roast. In fact, it was nothing more than a particular change of direction.

As for this light aid business, what she didn't understand was that I knew quite a bit about light aids. Most horses did. The difference was, we used our own playbook, and we used it primarily for training humans. A polite nudge against a human's shoulder illustrated a light aid that called for an apple or a ginger snap. Then we had the limp aid. Limping always sparked lively debate among humans. Even those who didn't know a limp from a lump offered advice on limping. These opinions ranged from which hoof was hiding an abscess to which old war injury caused a perfectly fit mare to favor her hip. Let me add here that the limp aid also worked for the horse that had enjoyed enough togetherness with his or her human. Why? Because the limp aid typically resulted in a bit of pasture rest, a cool drink of water, and extra oats for renewed strength. Creative limping could even stump a veterinarian. Spruce recently created a limp aid that resulted in getting his own paddock and a pleasant leave-of-absence. We horses knew a good deal about light aids, and we knew how to use them to train our humans.

Therefore, in the interest of fairness, it seemed that I should have been able to add my training methods to Madam's. Surely we could blend our ideas into an impartial agenda.

Let me offer an example of how my blended approach can work. This goes back to my antiviolence philosophy. Ever since my abrupt departure from the racetrack, I'd dismissed whips and rude training tools as annoying and highly impractical accessories. Early in our partnership, it became necessary to instruct Madam on this philosophy. The teaching moment came with one of those long whips that dressage aficionados keep handy. No doubt Madam paged through a Dover catalog and concluded she must have one of these accessories, only because everyone else had one. Fortunately for me, it took very little to change her mind about using it. For starters, she waved it around like a fly swatter. I simply ignored it. Each time she fumbled with the whip or gave me a snap, I did exactly nothing. Then, as fortune would have it, a favorite teacher of hers came to the farm for a weekend coaching session with the dressage queens. A man of sound good humor and judgment, David D. took one look at Madam brandishing that whip and asked if she was trying out for a role in *Mommy Dearest*. After that, good old David and I worked our magic on her. Each time she attempted to tweak me with the whip, he mentioned her resemblance to Cruella De Vil from *One Hundred and One Dalmatians* fame. Apparently, Mr. D used movies as teaching tools. Meanwhile, I simply hummed a Willy Nelson tune and pretended not to notice his gentle chiding. This all worked beautifully. Soon enough, Madam gave up on her clumsy lashing and took to slapping her own boot with the whip. All I do now is step on the gas and show a little pizzazz each time she whacks herself. This has worked out well for both of us.

As for the minor training impasse I mentioned earlier, it began with a trick called a "flying lead change." All horses knew how to do this, though some preferred a freestyle approach to a regimented method. A "lead" referred to which set of legs, left or right, led or reached forward farther than the other. This all happened when we canter or gallop. It was sort of a right hand/left hand thing. A "flying lead change" meant a horse moving at a canter or gallop would change from one lead to the other without slowing to a trot. In other words, the horse changed from one lead to the other in the air, thus the term "flying change."

Madam kept trying to convince me that a flying lead change should be smooth and elegant—back to this light aid business I mentioned earlier. Yet I don't fancy inhibiting my natural flow with this rather meek technique, and she hadn't warmed to my version. Admittedly, I added a little flourish to my style—and perhaps a smidge too much altitude. It just created more curb appeal for any spectators who might be on hand. I was sure it would give Madam a good chuckle, and it did—in the beginning. We were, however, a few months into this exercise, and she'd suddenly misplaced her funny bone.

Truthfully, I felt quite fresh during this morning's flying lead changes. And I guess I did squeal when she surprised me with those light aids again. Beyond that, I didn't understand the big to-do. I even made three or four lead changes all at once, which seemed like a better return on her investment than doing just one. I knew what came after one flying lead change—two flying lead changes. Then it was three or more. Why wait around for some lousy light aid to make it happen? Soon, she would ask me to perform many flying lead changes, all in a row. I simply skipped the middle part and showed her how this was done. As for the altitude business, my backside did not go an inch higher than the arena window. Nor did I strike the wall with my hind hoof, as was the case a week ago. This, by the way, did cause some excitement. The new summer shoes George fitted me with made quite a bang when they hit the steel arena wall. This launched a couple of runaways, including me. The shrieks that followed added drama, but only one person made an unplanned dismount, and she was just fine.

In any case, I've become extremely skilled at my version of this lead change, or leap change, as some have called it. Maybe with a little time, Madam also would learn to appreciate this extra embellishment to an otherwise boring maneuver.

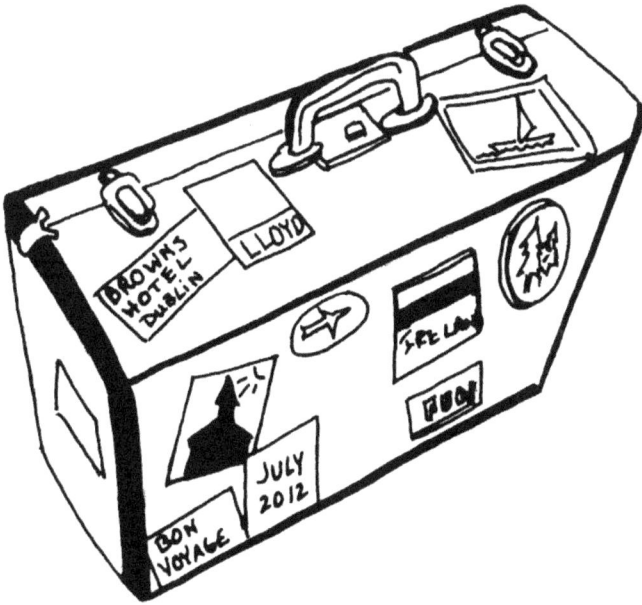

15

Off to the Emerald Isle

The weeks following our training debate found the management outlining some expectations surrounding our training program. Not that she criticized my approach, but she tightened the reins. Hence, it took some hard bargaining on my part to make it onboard the Aer Lingus flight to Ireland.

Mind you, the management protested loudly over forking out double airfare to include me. My continued unemployment meant I had little to offer to the travel budget except good behavior. That good behavior meant a promise from me to start applying myself to proper flying lead changes. That seemed like a fair agreement and certainly better than getting left at home. Actually, it was the only agreement available to me if I hoped to get on the plane to Dublin. As for the cost, I mentioned to Madam that my chilly seat assignment and lack of customer comforts might qualify for a reduced fare. But judging from the look on her face when she left the ticket counter, that argument didn't work. Aside from a queasy tummy on takeoff, my room in the cargo department worked out well enough. I simply spent seven hours napping and nibbling on Irish canapés, a far cry from my former life in red dirt country. None of my racing colleagues would believe this move from Oklahoma to Paddy's Pub in just a couple of months. Here we were, high in the air, on our way to a Celtic happening.

Once we landed in Dublin, Madam picked up our rental truck and an Irish version of my Comfy Sundowner trailer. I jumped in, and we motored out the gate toward Ballybungalo in County Laois. Incidentally, Madam's version of what might have been a restful, sightseeing drive should have required a strong seatbelt and a motion sickness bag for her passenger. Driving the Irish way on the opposite side of the road was not Madam's finest skill. Through my window, I could see Irish hounds, bikers, and even a few elderly hikers dive for safety in the blackberry bushes as we careened past—mostly in the wrong lane. Thankfully, we never encountered Irish law enforcement, though I could see people furiously punching numbers into their cell phones. Two hours of lurching through the countryside also left me with a bit of vertigo. It was a relief to arrive fairly unscathed at Ballybungalo, with only a few tree branches hanging off the Comfy Sundowner tailgate.

Our charming hosts trotted out the front door to greet us. They did seem surprised to see that Madam brought a horse for a traveling companion to such a splendid inn, but they couldn't have been more welcoming. After warm greetings, followed by refreshments, an agreeable fellow named Aengus escorted me to a walled garden behind the old hotel. This became my Irish home for the next few days. I paused before taking a stroll through the garden for fear of trampling heirloom tomatoes or a free-range hen. Madam never mentioned that our lodging involved a Regency mansion surrounded by formal gardens. Until now, the Dim

View Saloon comprised my dining and entertainment experience. Aengus immediately sensed my discomfort. He took off with the rental truck and trailer, returning an hour later with a new friend to help me settle into our posh lodgings. The new friend's name was Bob, and I could tell the moment we met that he and I would enjoy a grand time together.

While Madam toured the grounds and took in the Irish antiquities, Bob introduced me to a few of his chums. What a cheerful bunch. Over the next few days, it seemed to make little difference to any of them if it rained or if someone landed face first in the mud or lost a shoe or sprained an ankle dancing. Every day was a good day for Bob and his friends. Even the Ballybungalo chickens rallied with us when we hurtled past the hen house. They might not have laid many eggs afterward, but sprinting through the garden, flapping their wings, had to beat a dull day on a prickly nest. Our entourage of new mates kept increasing in size. Soon, we looked like a St. Paddy's Day parade. Bleating sheep, curious cattle, and an occasional draft horse lumbered behind us. We quite possibly enjoyed these outings more than did the neighbors. I noticed some towel-waving from kitchens windows as we passed, though we saw this as cheering for the team, not protests of our sightseeing tours.

It wasn't until we finished our third turn around the neighborhood that we met a couple of stern-looking farmers waiting near Bob's and my garden hideaway. One farmer had apprehended the draft horse, and the other clutched an indignant hen under his arm. Neither seemed enchanted to make our acquaintance. At this point, Bob suggested we slip off to the apple orchard and leave Aengus to make amends for our morning cavort. Aengus must have had the gift for gab because a touchy situation ended with handshakes and well-wishing all around. I couldn't help wondering where these sensible folks hid when we needed them to solve bigger problems.

Meanwhile, Madam also made a new friend, Caitlin. Caitlin looked after Bob's housing and grocery arrangements. Given the size of the lorry in which she squires him around, she must also have looked after Bob's stable mates. Each morning, she arrived at Ballybungalo village livery with a troop of wooly ponies, Irish draft horses, and a herding dog that came along for the ride. Caitlin announced she would like to escort Madam and me on a real Irish tour, not just a gallop around a municipal vegetable garden. She also proposed bringing Bob with us. But first, we again had to load up our supplies and ourselves in the Comfy Sundowner trailer. This time, Caitlin took the wheel. That afternoon, the four of us set out for another fancy abode, Castle Dare in County Clare. I thought that a place that featured a restaurant called the Earl of Thrice was not likely to offer lodging for the likes of Bob and me, but Caitlin insisted the Castle Dare help adored horses, even American quarter horses.

Castle Dare, like many grand Irish domiciles, was both elegant and old. They call it gothic revival style, though I might suggest it could have used more revival and less gothic. Bob and I once again were dispatched to a walled garden that served as our Castle Dare accommodation. This delightful equine retreat, built by a guy named Baron Von Inchiquine, featured the usual collection of rose bushes and manicured boxwood. The rest of the space gave us plenty of grazing and napping options. Best of all, Bob and I had a great view of a little lake just outside the garden. Castle Dare's concierge told us the lake held a great stock of rainbow trout, which prompted Madam and Caitlin to try their luck at fishing. Why they needed a fishing guide to troll around a teensy pond, I didn't know. But sure enough, a plump Irish ghillie named Jim showed up pondside. Jim planned to instruct them in how to snag a fish in what appeared to be an oversized fishbowl. It sounded easy. He also brought his entire collection of fishing paraphernalia.

Bob and I watched from our garden refuge, while the three of them scrambled into the boat and arranged all their gear. We could see that two anglers and a week's supply of food and gadgets presented a challenge for Jim. After securing all the loose items, he pushed the little dinghy away from shore, while managing to leave one of his Wellington boots behind in the muck. Bob and I agreed this was not an auspicious start to the girl's fly-fishing trip.

Once Jim guided the small craft to a promising fishing spot, he dropped anchor and commenced to assemble rods and bait. Madam and Caitlin, armed with their smartphone cameras, hung over the sides of the boat, attempting to photograph aquatic life. Neither showed much interest in catching fish, but they nearly succeeded in upending the boat. Eventually, Jim got the two outfitted. We overheard him sharing a few words of advice about keeping their lures out of one another's hair—a practical man.

Fortunately, the fishing—or at least the catching part—got off to a slow start. The first half hour produced nothing more than a clam that hitched a ride on Madam's line. Out came the smartphones to take advantage of this rare photo opportunity. Once everyone got resettled and tossed their lines back in the water, the action picked up. It started when Caitlin felt a small tug on her line. Jim immediately jumped to her aid, offering calm support as she waved her rod overhead and attempted to reel in her prize. Before she could get her line out of the water, she let out a shriek—she'd felt something more like a strike. Either she'd caught a second fish or caught the first fish twice. Nobody knew the answer to that question until she dragged the fish close enough to the boat for Jim to get a peek. Much to his dismay, he announced that Caitlin had caught a northern pike, not a rainbow trout.

The difference between the two begins with each fish's viewpoint on the world. If a rainbow has the disposition of a calico kitty, a northern qualifies as a mountain lion. A northern wields a mouthful of sharp teeth and the will to use them. Of course, Caitlin and Madam didn't know a pike from a pollywog, so they were not prepared for what happened next. Once Caitlin wangled her catch within Jim's reach, he could see she had two fish, a small rainbow—and a testy northern clinging to the smaller fish. Just about the time Caitlin engineered her trophy into the boat, the northern liberated the trout and crashed to the boat floor, furiously flopping under a seat. That's when the real event began. Soft-spoken Jim shouted that the girls needed to give the fish some space. Caitlin and Madam believed him but could see that space was at a premium in the tiny boat. The three of them proceeded to leap about the boat like a troupe of Irish dancers. Bob and I found this mysterious behavior pretty entertaining and began rooting for Caitlin. It was probably just as well nobody could hear us.

Soon, a handful of Castle Dare guests appeared at the window to inspect this production. A few braver souls approached the shore with their binoculars at the ready. The little boat now bobbed like a bathtub toy, as rods, nets, and food items tumbled overboard. Some observant rainbows quickly circled the ham sandwiches before they sank to the bottom. Caitlin and Madam, for their part, hopped from one seat to another, trying to avoid making contact with the pike's teeth. Jim made a valiant attempt to regain control of his boat and his belongings. It looked like a thankless job. After what must have seemed like an eternity to the anglers, Jim discovered a small bat among the remains of his tackle. With that, he made short work of subduing the pike. One would never have guessed such a harmless little cruise around a hotel pond could produce so much outstanding entertainment for so many observers.

Eventually, Jim guided the little dinghy back to shore with everyone still aboard, including both fish. The hotel guests discreetly drifted back to the dining room to finish their shepherd's pie. Madam and Caitlin stepped out of the boat, taking a minute to get their bearings as well as their balance. No surprise that Jim quickly gathered up his soggy belongings. He bid the two of them safe travels and high-tailed it for home—and probably his neighborhood pub. Bob and I made an executive decision that there would be no more fishing. Instead, the next day, the four of us would saddle up for a quiet hack through the countryside. Madam wanted to have a look at the neighbor's herd of Irish bog ponies anyway.

After two days of taking in the sights around County Clare, we loaded up again, relieved that nobody had flattened a hen or come to a bad end in Castle Dare pond. Bob and I again jumped into the Comfy Sundowner, and the four of us aimed for County Kerry. Caitlin obviously understood Irish roads and drivers better than Madam, so the trip went more smoothly than the one from Dublin. We arrived just in time for the Puck Fair, an ancient three-day celebration held in Killorglin.

Some call this the Fair of the Goat, as it involves a bunch of over-served pub customers hiking up into the mountains to capture a wild goat. Why a goat? I'm not sure but maybe because it represents Pan, the pagan god of shepherds and flocks. That seemed like a good enough reason to celebrate anyway. And judging from the tippling and dancing that went on at the Puck Fair, good old Pan must have been a partying kind of guy. Once the pub customers returned with a goat, they dolled it up with ribbons and hoisted it up on a platform above the village square. That's when the merriment officially began. As for little goat gruff, he got pampered for a couple of days before being crowned King Puck. Nothing about this reminded me of the Minnesota state fair, though Bob and I did see it as an opportunity to meet a few "traveler" girls of gypsy origin.

We arrived on opening day, just in time for the horse fair—good news for Bob and me. I planned to check out a Kerry bog pony, like the ones we visited at Castle Dare. We learned these ponies were once used to haul peat from the bogs, and they would be competing in a peat-hauling contest here at the Puck Fair. We just passed a farmer leading three such ponies down the road toward the celebration. Aengus from Ballybungalo told me these tiny ponies' distant relatives played a role in defeating Napoleon at Waterloo in 1815. I found this hard to believe, given their diminutive size, but it made a good story. It also occurred to me that we had room in the trailer to bring a pony back to the States with us.

Meanwhile, due to the large crowd, Madam parked our rig in a field about a half mile from the village. Bob and I tidied up, while she and Caitlin chatted with some unruly children eating their breakfast by the walking path. The four of us then marched to the village, where serious celebration was well underway. Farmers trotted their sale horses in twos and threes through the mob, scattering fair visitors in their wake. Young men raised their glasses of Guinness, singing and toasting pretty much everything. An ancient teamster scrubbed his draft horses in the river that flowed through the village center. Shopkeepers danced with visitors, while the decorated goat presided cheerfully from his platform above the throng. Bob and I must have looked to the partygoers like tall tourists. We also must have looked available to ride—or perhaps to purchase! And another thing, Bob fielded more than a few smacks on the rear from flirtatious mares cruising through the horse auction. While I love a party, and Bob and I did discuss meeting Irish girls, we Minnesotans tend to party Scandinavian style, with a slice of apple pie and a cup of black coffee. It's a restrained version that does not include a goat for a centerpiece. Well, maybe if you're a Saint Paul Saints baseball fan, you could encounter a captured goat, but only for a single ballgame, and it probably would be dressed in a running suit.

Jeez oh me, after a couple of hours and a few fistfights, we witnessed a remarkable incident. A small fellow and a full-bodied woman, twirling away to traditional Irish music, suddenly dropped out of sight. Over the riverbank, they sashayed. Stranger yet, they landed in the midst of the draft-horse bathing project. The unexpected dancers definitely caught the old teamster and his half-bathed horses by surprise. Just about the time he and the capsized twirlers untangled themselves from one another, the draft team cleared the top of the bank at a dead run. Meanwhile, the crowd parted like the Red Sea, making room for the startled horses. After clearing the dance area, the team disappeared through the trees and into a nearby forest. The ancient teamster and the dancers wobbled up the bank to survey the damage. Madam and Catlin stayed just long enough to see that nobody suffered any life-threatening injuries. Aside from some spilled Guinness and a few bruises, everyone appeared to be in one piece. At that point, Caitlin decided we had seen enough of the Puck Fair for one day.

Bob and I offered no resistance. Between the bawdy Irish mares and the ill-fated dancers, we agreed it was time to head back to the Comfy Sundowner. But first, we wanted to check out the woods where the draft team had made such a dramatic exit. I let Bob go first, afraid we might encounter something unpleasant. At the speed those bad boys were traveling, they could have flattened a small building. But that wasn't the case. Instead, they galloped down a lane, dragging their harness traces behind them. Miraculously, nothing got entangled, and neither horse fell. Instead, the two took their ease in a lovely pond, surrounded by lush grazing opportunities. They looked like a couple of moose sunbathing in a Canadian swamp. Apparently, these two really enjoyed water and might have stayed in the river all day, had the dancers not surprised them.

Bob and I introduced ourselves to the twosome and asked if they needed our help.

"No, thanks," replied the biggest horse. "We'll just cool off for a while and then find our way home. It's going to take a couple of days for those dancers to settle down."

We said our good-byes and left the runaways to their lunch. Since we saw no sign of their owner, we assumed the horses were accustomed to finding their own way home.

"He made a good point," I said to Bob, as we walked through the woods toward the Comfy Sundowner. "That Puck Fair might go on for a few days. But I'll have to give them credit. Those two were awfully calm after such a brouhaha."

"Yup," replied Bob. "That's the Irish way—calm after the brouhaha. That's not the first time those horses have had to find their own way home from a party."

I already was afraid to learn what our next tour destination might be.

"It's Tralee," proclaimed Caitlin with gusto when we met her at the trailer. "I managed to get us four tickets to the Rose of Tralee Festival."

I didn't know anything about the Rose of Tralee, but we were greatly relieved when she assured us the Rose of Tralee carnival and parade involved no goats or river dancers.

16

The Mystery of Women, Horses, and Food

As much as I enjoyed touring Ireland with Bob and Caitlin, it was great to be home. Even Madam seemed relieved to wave good-bye to our enchanting hosts and climb aboard the old Airbus headed for Minnesota. When we arrived at Evergreen, things looked about the way they had when we left two weeks ago. Ghillie still was snoozing under his favorite linden tree. Of course, he wanted to know all about the Puck Fair and the Irish bog ponies. Andres still was shy but he did speak a few words of Spanish to me. He probably was just testing to see if my vocabulary had improved. I'd been trying to learn enough Spanish so I could converse a bit and understand a few Span-ish jokes. According to Bingo, a few more newcomers arrived in our absence—all female. And that usually meant their human partners were female too. Women and their horses—it was a curious thing that governed most stables.

Fortunately for us horses, the attraction began at an early age and often lasted a lifetime. This was good, because according to the TV news blaring away in Evergreen's front office, we needed lots of women to solve the world's problems. I didn't know an upside-down mortgage from a 401(k), but I did know that women seemed to figure out how to make things run right

Women typically solved their conflicts without the use of a lot of foul language or firearms—well, maybe a few off-color jokes now and then, but basically, I heard women around here speaking in pretty cordial tones. Law-abiding, good-natured, carrot-packing partners—that's how I would describe them. Not only did the Evergreen women play well together, but they also seemed to know how to get along with tricky horses. And when I say tricky, I'm speaking of horses with sketchy pasts and shady reputations. You know the kind—the racehorse that broke up starting gates. Or how about the trail boss that refused to leave the barn or that made a break for home when his rider tried to eat the sandwich she'd packed for the road. I'm also talking about the show jumper who stopped to let his rider clear the fence first. It was amazing how many horses started their careers on the wrong path, only to get straightened out by a patient woman who managed to have her say with them.

Show me a cow horse that's bored with cattle, and I'll find you a woman who can change his mind. Let me also mention the reluctant dressage prospect that meets a helpful female. In no time, this problem student is crazy about full bridles and performing half passes. It's true. Call it a knack for diplomacy or plain old determination, but women know a lot about changing a horse with a bad attitude into a winning partner and a fine cribbage player. I've actually seen a woman teach a cranky Clydesdale to smile and play Texas Hold'em.

Women also know how to manage complicated situations around the barn. Take the landlord, for example. Instead of whining about her tenants' annoying habits, she organized us so we now room next door to our favorite Horseopoly partners. This definitely reduced the number of irritable neighbor complaints. Then, there was Omar's partner, Monica, who could sew up a ruined Rambo blanket as quickly as my friend Patrick can shred it. Resourceful, that's what women are.

Women presided at Evergreen, and there was a back-story to this. Most Evergreen women enjoyed riding as children. Then, along came school and maybe a marriage or a career, and horses exited from their lives. After a timeout to train their mates and motivate their children, these women often decided to come back to the barn for another go at the horses. Once this happened, most of them would ride forever, or at least as long as they could hoist themselves into the saddle and sit upright. This was the case at Evergreen—mature women hoisting themselves into the saddle and attempting to remain upright.

I suspect that horse partnerships also provided women a perfect antidote to a midlife crisis. For women who can't afford to travel the world to seek their bliss, and discover their untapped passions, a diplomatic horse makes a perfect midlife sounding board. We make perfect travel companions as well. And we make excellent conversationalists and pleasant dinner dates. Just ask Madam about our Irish tour. Not a discouraging word was exchanged on the entire trip—with the exception of the Castle Dare fishing incident, which fortunately did not include me.

But it's more than mature women who find us horses irresistible. It's young girls, the ones who later become the presiding women. Almost every horse establishment entertains plenty of girls. Boys may start riding with boundless enthusiasm, but they often fizzle, once organized sports come into play. As far as I can tell, though, girls mostly stick with horses—not fussy girls who worry about fashion and gossip but the ones who show up at the barn dressed in pink flowered tights and Ugg boots. These girls like to gallop bareback over garbage can jumps just for the heck of it. Girls who tend to stick with horses for a lifetime also like to have fun racing their ponies and taking them for a swim in the neighbor's pond. Since horse-crazy girls choose to spend countless hours at the stable, they might also entertain themselves by dressing Madam's elderly Jack Russell in a Peter Pan outfit. Or they've been known to tie a sunbonnet on Olivia's goat Bella, just to see how long it takes Bella to eat the hat.

Girls who came to Evergreen's horse camp might accidently put a bridle on upside down, or they might forget a bridle all together. Saddles seemed to be an inconvenience for many of them, especially when an old towel made a fine seating arrangement. We never heard girls complain that the ground was too wet or lumpy to ride. And they didn't carp about having headaches or that the radio was playing loud Kenny Chesney music. They ate the stale cookies from Evergreen's lunchroom as if they'd never tasted anything so delectable. They decorated the cat's box and shared their lunches with the pet rabbits living in the indoor arena. They provided lots of entertainment for the rest of us.

Maybe the thing I liked best about Evergreen's girls was that starting at about age eight, they pretended to be horses. They'd whinny to one another. They'd shake their ponytails and squeal. They'd also pretend to be jockeys and polo players. These misses also liked to dress up their ponies. Mane braiding with ribbons was especially popular. I saw quite a few pink hooves, as well as glitter sprinkled on pony butts. It was a matter of taste, but mostly it was a matter of fun.

I'd like to return to the subject of females and food. A stable is likely to be home to not just a bunch of women but a bunch of food-ies. These women know their way around the kitchen. Now, this is not to say women belong in the kitchen. Women belong anywhere they choose to be, whether it's the Old Country Buffet salad line or the Supreme Court. Yet I happen to know that Madam and her friends have spent many an hour parading around their kitchens, turning out fabulous food. Sometimes they even turned out fabulous horse treats that magically appeared in my room. Coffee cakes and Snickerdoodles regularly passed my front door on their way to Evergreen's lunch table. Although Madam recently suggested I was getting rather rotund, I've had some good help getting there.

All this leads me to a topic we visit daily at our house: signing up for cooking classes. Not classes that teach how to make lima-bean casseroles or tater tots. I want to learn how to make and bake the good stuff—kid-tested, horse-friendly birthday food. Come to think of it, a good cooking class combined with my new foreign language skills could land me in another career opportunity! Of course, these brain-storms of mine require a bit of assistance from my assistant, if you catch my drift. Not only is she sterling on the keyboard, but Madam also knows a thing or two about operating the KitchenAid mixer and all those wooden spoons.

17

No Bullying

If I thought the raving talk radio caused a guy to feel gloomy, something equally unfriendly turned up at Evergreen Farm— bullying. I assumed this happened only in dank and dreary places, not at a charming abode such as ours. It didn't set well with me, especially when someone made unkind jokes about my friend's big feet or poked fun if someone else didn't make the hoofleball team. Maybe it was a way for small individuals to feel big.

On the morning when Gabe reported that some roughnecks down the road had been making fun of Omar, it set me to stewing. One might not guess by his size, but Omar frightens easily. He's a softy and doesn't always stand up for himself. According to Gabe, the snarky guys called Omar "Uncle Oomph," as he tended to avoid strenuous exercise. That made my hair stand on end. They even sent Omar an e-mail saying he couldn't run the length of an Evergreen paddock, even if his lunch depended on it.

It was true that Omar was a tad portly, a detail that could slow him down and discourage him from signing up for aerobics class. He looked strong and handsome under saddle, but he wasn't exactly buff either—his silhouette could have used a tune-up. I'll also admit Omar was afraid of thunder and worried about rogue cats leaping out of the tack room to grab him by the ankle. Well, for Pete's sake, we all have worried about that since the day Snuggles chased a chipmunk up my leg.

I wondered to myself why would these bullies get all worked up over a kindly fellow like Omar. Maybe they took offense to his unusual clothes. He did have a unique wardrobe, though most of us thought he looked grand in his purple polo wraps and slinky underwear. He was white, after all, and the undies provided after-bath protection from unsightly stains.

None of Omar's flaws gave anyone the right to pick on him. In fact, I intended to have a word with those bad boys. Little did they know I could open gates and track them directly to their messy man cave. Come to think of it, I just might write a letter about this ugly incident to the editor of the *Maple Plain Gazette*!

Meanwhile, I told Omar to turn off his laptop and forget the e-mail business. He wasn't too computer savvy anyway, and I saw no reason for him to read any more rude messages. Besides which, those hooligans knew nothing about Omar except that he was big and sort of fluffy. They had no idea he ranked number one in the best-friend department. He was a guy who shared his organic carrots and laughed at all our jokes. He also was good-natured about joining me on tour in the Comfy Sundowner, even when I didn't tell him where we were going. It was great to have a pal who always said yes whenever I asked him to do something new. No matter if I suggested a drive to the Scott County fair or a garden tour on Lake Minnetonka, good old Omar always agreed to give it a whirl.

What's more, he never spoke unkindly of Spruce and the other oldsters who sang off-key and sometimes got lost in the pasture. He never laughed when someone stumbled over the cavaletti poles. He was an impeccable host, even when that petulant pony Prince joined us for a round of cards. And then there was the time Omar accompanied me to a movie on Evergreen Date Night, when neither of us had a date. Of course, Omar always played a sharp game of gin rummy.

I wonder what the bullies would say if I invited them over for a little gin rummy tournament. We could offer a prize to add incentive to the proposal. Maybe Madam could whip up a batch of her peanut butter horse treats. Those guys just might agree to come if we concocted delectable appetizers, such as a keg of apple cider and my newest baking achievement—apple spice cake! Maybe they would like a batch of apple tarts from Dumas Orchard. I'd bet once Omar showed them how he wins at gin rummy, they'd sing a different tune. Next thing we'd know, he'd be captain of their skijoring team. He was a big strong guy; all he needed was a little encouragement and a shot of self-confidence.

After mulling over this brainstorm, I decided to present my idea to Omar. It would be important to catch him when he was feeling calm and relaxed, so I picked an afternoon when he and the rest of our card club typically relaxed in the pasture. Just as Omar started closing his eyes, I offhandedly suggested the gin rummy solution. He did not exactly jump for joy.

"I don't care to meet those guys," he muttered. "Why would we want to play cards with them anyway? They probably don't even know how to count cards, much less play them. And food? You mean to say you want to waste Mrs. Dumas's sweet tango tarts on those dumbbells?"

"Good point," I agreed. "I was just thinking of ways we might come to a neighborly agreement or at least discuss neighborly etiquette."

"Etiquette schmetiquette," he groused from behind drooping eyelids.

"Well, what if we invited them over, and they ended up apologizing for their bad behavior?" I asked. "We'll never know if we never speak to them."

"Maybe," Omar replied, seemingly unconvinced.

Oh my. Maybe this wasn't the brightest idea after all—a party for the enemy. *Oh well*, I thought as I looked at my friend snoozing in the sunshine. It was then that I noticed an unfamiliar face peeping from behind some blackberry bushes in a nearby pasture. It was a small bay mare, and a rather attractive one at that. I could see she had a pair of binoculars around her neck. She appeared to be spying on us. *Well, what now?* Was she on a reconnaissance mission of some kind? And if so, what the heck was she looking for? "Where did that powder puff come from?" I wondered out loud. I also wondered how long she had been listening to our conversation.

Omar opened one eye, cast a sleepy glance in Powder Puff's direction, and quickly coasted back to dreamland. The lurker happened to be occupying the bully pasture, or so I thought, based on Gabe's account. Could this be a member of the bully team? Me o my, maybe they didn't know how to write so they sent a girl to take notes for them.

"Well, well, what have we here?" I whispered to the dozing Omar. "It's time for a closer look."

Powder Puff could tell I noticed her, though she stood her ground, making no attempt to get away. This pint-sized peeper behaved rather boldly, which of course piqued my interest. I seemed to suffer from an attraction to bold women. In any case, easing toward the fence, I ticked through a list of icebreaking techniques for meeting girls.

"Ahem," I intoned, using my best debating voice.

"Ahem yourself," Powder Puff replied abruptly, before I had a chance to toss out a witty icebreaker.

Oh boy, it looks like another one of those *females*, I thought, observing her slightly curled lip. "And what brings you to our pasture fence?" I mildly inquired.

She only offered her name—Emma. Not Emma Johnson or Emma from Chicago—just Emma.

"Well, Emma, what can I do for you today?" I asked, keeping it light.

She cleared her throat as if to speak but seemed to change her mind and said nothing.

"My name is Noah, and I manage this pasture," I continued smoothly. "I also serve as director of Evergreens' welcoming committee."

"Oh, I know all about you," she replied, catching me off balance. "I also know all about Gabe, and Copper and Omar." At that point, Emma presented a list of embarrassing details she had collected about each of us. She mentioned a few specifics, such as who rolled daily in manure and who snored the loudest. Then she added a couple of more delicate details, like who burped while he ate his lunch and which one of us coughed without covering his mouth. She even mentioned that Omar passed a little gas now and then.

"I sincerely hope you don't plan to post these details on any Internet dating sites," I retorted, keeping my cool. Her commentary about my pasture mates was starting to sound vaguely familiar. If memory served, some of her points appeared in an earlier e-mail that arrived in Omar's mailbox. "So, Emma," I continued cautiously. "What interests you about my friends? Do you run a personal coaching clinic or a Mr. Manners business?"

"No," she replied crisply. "I'm just curious about how guys act when we girls aren't around. Well, it also could be that I'm looking for someone to invite on a trail ride next weekend," she added. "It's an invitational trail ride along the St. Croix River, and I need to bring a date."

If it's a date she's looking for, I thought, *she certainly picked an odd way to get acquainted.*

"Do you have someone in mind?" I persisted. "You know, there are lots of ways to meet new friends other than recording their burps and bathing habits. How is it you happen to be shopping in our territory?"

"I'm not shopping," she snapped. "I'm just observing. And besides, most of you guys are stinky—all except the big white fellow over there sleeping. He's manages to stay cleaner than the rest of you because he wears that slinky underwear."

Hah. I was beginning to understand where this conversation was headed. No thanks to Gabe, but our bullying mystery might be coming to light right here and now. It seemed our girl Emma was nursing a crush on Omar. Could she actually be the bully? Maybe I wouldn't have to face off with her older brothers after all, which struck me as a safer plan.

"Emma," I asked, "do you know that in addition to passing gas, several of us bake?"

"Well, that's pretty hard to believe," she countered.

"And by the way, I enjoy Spanish classes and shopping at the farmer's market, as does my friend Omar." She looked wary. "Oh, and we all travel. I recently toured Ireland, not to mention Wisconsin. In fact, we plan to take a road trip to Montana and a visit few national parks soon. Plus, my friends often accompany me to library ribbon cuttings and polka dances. Why, just last week we marched in the Maiden Rock Summer Fest parade. And one last thing: we enjoy playing cards. And speaking of cards, why don't you join us for a hand or two of Canasta?"

Emma thought this over before offering a tentative, "Only if you leave the gate open." She must have been worried that we would tie her up and take her captive.

"There is just one small detail," I added. "You must first apologize to Omar for the unkind e-mail you sent him."

She looked uneasy. "What e-mail? I don't even know Omar. Besides, he looks big enough to take care of himself," she said defensively.

"Ah, but Omar is my friend, and this is our pasture. You're welcome here but only if you play by our rules," I explained. "You're the one who hurt his feelings. If you want to meet him, you can begin by getting to know him. But it starts with an apology."

Emma squirmed, but she did not run. In fact, she finally agreed to do as I asked and meet our herd for a friendly round of cards. The good news—Omar felt much better about himself. Furthermore, none of our bios showed up on Match.com. We also scheduled another card game, including Powder Puff.

18

Ghillie on YouTube

Madam arrived early at Evergreen. The local TV meteorologist had predicted hot weather, and she was packing a bunch of towels and a bucket. Obviously, someone was about to get a bath, though I hoped that someone was not yours truly. I happened to enjoy the suit of mud that I'd acquired yesterday and did not look forward to a major scrub this early in the day.

My worries were unfounded. By the time Andres delivered my breakfast, Madam had delivered Ghillie to the Evergreen spa, where he was about to get a good laundering, with help from my fabulous silk shampoo. While I was happy to share hair products with Ghillie, I had to wonder what prompted this sudden interest in hygiene before breakfast. Fortunately, my room offered good viewing of Evergreen's spa services. *I should be able to learn what's on today's agenda*, I thought.

Ghillie still looked a mite peaked. Maybe he'd added a few pounds over the past month but not nearly enough. His eyes looked brighter, though, and his coat held a bit of a shine. *The silk shampoo and conditioner ought to boost that a bit*, I thought. On a scale of one to ten in the wellness department, I would give him about a four. It was hard to believe, in his condition, that he would sign on for a hair appointment. Madam must have convinced him that what he needed was a good dose of soap and water. Or maybe she just wanted to show me the value of sharing my personal belongings, including my shampoo and detangling goo. I could hardly wait to hear what the two of them had planned.

According to Madam, the University of Minnesota's veterinary faculty made an appointment to film Ghillie for a fund-raising video. The purpose of this little endeavor was to document success stories of horses that landed in the university's large animal clinic. The fact that Ghillie spent weeks in their critical care unit and lived to talk about it made him an ideal candidate for this video. That, plus he was a fine fellow and would capture lots of attention on YouTube.

His Lyme disease, followed by his kidney failure, followed by multiple health crises after that could have made him just another complicated veterinary case. But I learned that Ghillie was one of those brave, quiet types who wins hearts. Watching him improved my technique for meeting girls. Not that Ghillie needed a date. He seemed to charm everyone with his sincere questions and genuine interest in their answers. According to Madam, even when he could hardly lift his head off the floor, Ghillie welcomed vet students for a visit. By all accounts, the clinic staff fell hard for him.

Madam finished his bath, dried him off, and parked him in the grooming stall next to me, where we could enjoy a little chat. "What do you think about this YouTube production?" I asked him. "Do you suppose they expect you to tell a few jokes or wear a hat? I have plenty of hats you can borrow."

"Hardly," Ghillie replied with a half smile. "I think they just want a little family reunion with a few photos. My guess is they're all curious to see if I'm still standing upright and taking nourishment," he chuckled.

Sure enough, within the hour a small army of university folks showed up at Evergreen. They carried cameras, tripods, cookies, and a handsome leather halter with a brass plate bearing Ghillie's name. It looked as if most of the school decided to join the production as they spilled through Evergreen's front door. I'm talking professors, vet techs, a massage therapist, a handful of students, and even my favorite farrier George, who just happened to show up. George, by the way, had managed Ghillie's feet since he came home from the university. The landlords quickly retrieved a bunch of folding chairs and some refreshments for the occasion. Ghillie's primary vet, a third-year student, snapped photos, while the massage therapist gave him a quick rubdown for old time's sake.

All this got me thinking about the theme of their video production—success. One look at Ghillie didn't really shout success. All those vets and teachers knew how to figure out serious health problems, so I guess that meant success. They also knew how to rehabilitate a guy like Ghillie with drugs and nutrition. I'd call that quite an achievement as well. An injured horse returning to the racetrack also spelled success. From what I could tell, all those students invested lots of dollars and hours learning skills that helped them succeed in their work. It sort of made me wonder what old Ghillie thought about success.

He seemed to be making slow progress, though he sure struggled to get around. He said his feet hurt. Actually, I'd never seen him move faster than a walk, and even that looked pretty painful. Yet he seemed content, dozing quietly under his favorite linden tree. And he really liked watching the Evergreen hoofleball team play. Those might be small successes, but it was hard to believe he would ever again walk onto a racetrack or into a show ring. Madam said she had many questions about his future. He already had suffered one relapse when they gave him his spring inoculations. Plus, he sometimes appeared to be short of breath. Other days, he politely pointed out that he would rather not talk to me. I'd even seen him stop in the driveway, as if to say to Madam, "How about passing on the exercise for today?" But of course, even I was known to try that little scam.

Everyone in our card club asked me why Madam kept

hanging in there with Ghillie. "Wouldn't it have been easier for her to put him down and be done with it?" asked Copper.

"Easier, maybe; better, I'm not sure," I offered. "According to her, each time they treated him for one thing or another, he responded well. His kidneys improved. His appetite perked up. His shoulder healed after falling in his stall. What do you do when a guy seems to be getting better?"

Nobody knew what to say, though we all agreed that Ghillie continued to gain strength and appeared to enjoy life in a modest way. He even liked a little walk in the park. It was the ongoing hoof problems that worried Madam. His X-rays drew concerned expressions from everyone who understood life-altering lameness.

Madam said the real problems began when she brought Ghillie home from the university. One year and thousands of hours of personal care later, "We just kept walking forward," she said. "He slowly improved over the course of that year, but we never really had any perfect answers."

She'd made a mighty big commitment when she signed on for that. After hearing the whole story, it was hard not to wonder why.

"Well," she said, "whether we're ending an important relationship, or leaving a job, or choosing a career, or even deciding to continue care for someone we love, most of us try hard to make good decisions. We can only do this based on what we know. At that point, we have to come to peace with the outcome of our choices."

Goodness, I thought. *I hope she considers me someone she loves!*

Just about then, Madam excused herself and went off to talk with the landlords about extension cords for the movie crew. This gave me a moment to speak to Ghillie, who was looking somewhat refreshed from his bath.

"Um, Ghillie, what do you think about this movie business?" I queried, hoping my question was not too personal. He always smiled when I asked him things like this. "What I mean is, I can see you're feeling better, but do you really feel like a success story?" Oh dear, that might not have been a good choice of words. "Maybe it's the word success that bothers me," I dithered. "So far, my own achievements have been pretty much invisible. Some days it feels like I'm just chasing girls and testing new careers without accomplishing much." There was silent reflection on his part—or was he ignoring me? "Can I tell you about something that happened this week that felt a little like success?" I asked

"Go for it," he replied, turning his gaze my way.

With any luck, Madam would give us a few minutes alone. I mentioned to Ghillie how some unfriendly activity had turned up at Evergreen Farm last week—bullying.

Ghillie frowned. "Continue," he said.

"Gabe told me he thought some rough neighbors might have been making fun of Omar. Gabe also reported that these toughs called Omar an unkind name and sent him dumb e-mail messages. All I know is, it hurt Omar's feelings."

Ghillie listened without comment.

"So I had this idea. I decided to invite the bullies over to play gin rummy. Omar happens to be very good at gin rummy, you know. He would have cleaned their clocks and had them begging him to manage their slow-pitch softball team. But then something happened that turned everything upside down," I explained.

"Go on," said Ghillie.

"I discovered it wasn't a bunch of thugs pestering Omar. It was a girl. A girl with a crush on him!" I checked to see that Ghillie was still listening. He was. "Anyway, I introduced myself to her, had a few words, and invited her to join us in a card game. She admitted to sending Omar the stinky notes and claimed she was trying to meet him and couldn't figure out how to get his attention."

Ghillie looked puzzled. "Odd," he remarked. Ghillie only said more when his comments needed clarification.

"But that's not all," I said. "I insisted she apologize to Omar first. 'No apology, no introduction' was what I told her. She seemed pretty upset about the whole matter, but she finally did it."

"How did Omar do with her apology?" Ghillie asked.

"Honestly, he seemed more amazed to learn a girl wanted to meet him than concerned about her apology," I said. "By the time she finished making amends, old Omar must have forgotten the whole thing. So what do you think?"

"I think that story shows a splendid success," said Ghillie. "For everyone."

That's when Madam and the landlord returned to finish Ghillie's hair and makeup for the big production.

The camera crew and university friends eventually settled in to watch the interview and filming. I was hoping for an introduction to the photographer and maybe a word with someone about filming our hoofleball team for a YouTube promotion, but they all were pretty busy listening to the interviewer and admiring Ghillie. He just hung out behind Madam, twirling her hair with his lips and nudging her to move this production business along. That morning, he looked more like a bored thoroughbred wanting to get to work than a miraculous patient recovering from a life-threatening illness. He scanned the pasture for any trespassing deer. Then he attempted to interview the cameraman by sticking his snoot into the lens. For that brief moment, Ghillie showed every sign of health. I remembered then what Madam told me about her childhood friend Bob Stall.

"He simply enjoyed being with his horses, conversing with them, negotiating with them, and sharing the passage of time together." I was beginning to understand what she meant.

After everyone left, Madam turned Ghillie out into his paddock with the favorite linden tree. She stood for several minutes at the gate, probably wondering once more whether she'd made the right decision. Would he ever really recover, or would he spend his days shuffling around and sunning himself? Maybe it didn't matter.

I'm sure I heard her ask him if he would like to take a few months off to relax in an apple orchard with some good-humored broodmares.

His answer, though I couldn't quite hear it, felt to me like yes.

19

Age Advantage

Anybody who has made the acquaintance of a Jack
Russell terrier knows the meaning of "in charge." Wally of Evergreen
Farm, for example, managed to wheedle his way into a woodworking
business. He then clawed a path to the top-dog position of chief executive
officer. (By the way, Wally lands just north of baby boomer when it
comes to age.) It certainly was an interesting career path to watch. But
then, I probably didn't qualify as an expert on career paths.

Not that I disliked Jack Russell terriers. In fact, I found them
quite fascinating, in a master sergeant sort of way. In my estimation,

they got an A+ for their human management skills. They even provided excellent case studies for those of us entering the human management field. It also happened that we maintained an overachieving Jack Russell in our household. I'm speaking of Madam's elderly Jack Russell, Ms. Mouse, who insisted on crisscrossing the state with Madam and the Fluff Muffin Cat. This petite curmudgeon was well past the baby boomer age group. Her face might be white, and her body parts didn't mesh as well as they once did, but this old girl still knew a thing or two about management. That included management of our entire family.

Madam should have seen this cheeky personality when she plucked Mouse from the litter nearly thirteen years ago. At twelve weeks old, this pup took up governing everyone, from her littermates to the family hamster. She tolerated no flimflam, then or now. Sanitation crews and mail carriers, beware! Grandmothers walking lap dogs had better gird their loins when they passed the house. The barks could be deafening. Madam recently asked a house painter for a painting bid. He stopped over the next day. and finding nobody at home, he strolled around the outside of the house, making notes. He then called and left the following message:

"Hullo, Madam. I have your painting bid for you. I also wanted to let you know that your home is safe from burglars. My point is, if I ain't been able to see that dog, I'd a-still been a runnin'!" Not only did Mouse express more opinions than a presidential candidate, she cultivated this art as she grew older. Her age-related ploys were so effective that I thought maybe I should start fibbing about *my* age and try to use this as a bargaining chip. *No, I don't want to be a youngster again, though that might appeal to some of the debutant mares that keep moving into Evergreen.* I was just realizing that age enjoyed certain benefits, and Ms. Mouse took pleasure in many of those benefits. For example, she often appeared at Evergreen decked out in stylish new apparel. Sometimes it was a sleek jacket from Louis and Luigi's Pet Emporium. Other days, it was a sparkly collar from Bloomingtails. I also saw her reclining in Madam's office chair. This ploy resulted in Madam giving the ergonomically correct chair to the dog. She then went searching for a folding chair as a substitute. The dog won.

Mouse would give no more than a sigh and a look of pending starvation, and her supper would appear on her personalized placemat. No ordinary supper, mind you, but one dressed with homemade chicken and brown rice casserole and topped off with a dab of Earth's Best organic baby food!

When she was not adorning Madam's office chair, Mouse lounged on a luxurious throne designed for a St. Bernard. Incidentally, both Ms. Mouse and the Fluff Muffin Cat have hijacked Madam's bed. Madam now camps on the sofa, where she can straighten her legs and rest her head on something besides fur. When she's tried to share the bed with the hairballs, she's been forced to sleep horizontally. Both pets enjoyed complete comfort and plenty of room to stretch out. It seemed like I should be learning something from these examples.

Let me mention another example of seniors with benefits, Ms. Mouse's best friend, the Princely Poodle. Every day, he tottered through the Victoria Dog Park, greeting guests and signing autographs for adoring labradoodles. His selective hearing helped him sidestep most human commands and all rules of etiquette. He often was seen pilfering garbage cans and browsing kitchen counters. He even helped himself to Madam's cappuccino while on a road recent trip up north. Generally, the Princely Poodle made tasteful food choices, though he once ate a bar of soap, resulting in an emergency trip to the vet.

All this convinced me that these oldsters would make perfect lobbyists for AARP. I also was convinced that a horse might pull this aging ruse. I could manufacture a slight limp just to test the process. Or maybe a nagging cough would work, though somebody would probably fill my feed bucket with lousy hay cubes. (That's what coughing horses get instead of fresh hay.) Maybe it would be worth trying a few gray highlights in my mane.

Come to think of it, old Spruce from down the aisle might be able to help me out. He was the right age to understand this kind of thing. On the other hand, it also was possible he wouldn't remember who I am!

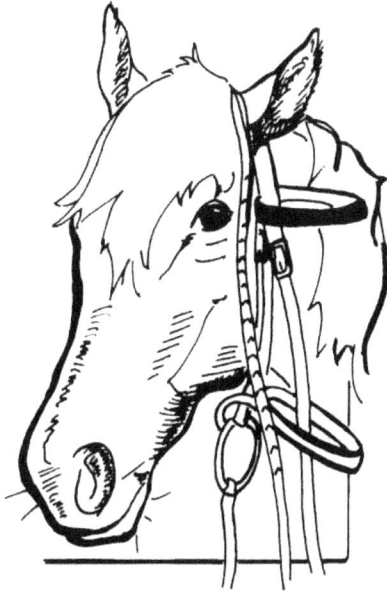

20

Touring in the Comfy Sundowner

We'd marched in plenty of parades and even attended a rutabaga festival this summer. Between the Memorial Day band concert and Lake City Eagle Days, I'd developed a sudden urge to start playing the trombone. Madam added an extra floor mat to my Comfy Sundowner, due to a nasty case of blisters I'd developed at last week's Barnes PRCA Rodeo. She told me these excursions introduced me to new sites and sounds that could make me into the "bombproof" partner she'd dreamed of. All this road trip training must have related to our Baker Park incident with the alien Rollerblader. Ever since that day, she'd been crowing

about personal safety—her personal safety, mind you. "How can I
operate as your editorial assistant when you bolt
at the sight of a black-capped chickadee. What if I take another header
into the shrubs?" she inquired. "All I need is a fractured collar bone, and
you, my dear fellow, will find yourself enrolled in a typing class."

Um ... I think not.

We were "on the road again," as Willie Nelson would sing,
heading to the Wisconsin border to take in more of those bomb-
proofing sights and sounds Madam kept talking about. Today's outing
began with a drive through the countryside to the teeny town of El
Paso, Wisconsin. Here we immersed ourselves into the World
Champion Bacon Festival. The highlight of the morning: a parade
hosted by the El Paso Chamber of Commerce and led by a portly
woman dressed in a bacon costume. As for the parade entries, I liked
the Toro lawnmower drill team and a hand-decorated manure spreader
filled with local city council members. If this was any indication of
the day's activities, count me in.

After dining on a BLT for breakfast, Madam climbed into her
trusty Ram truck, and we zipped off to the village of Elmwood, the UFO
capital of the world (or at least of Wisconsin). Madam said the town
earned that title a few years back when local law enforcement officers
spotted an unidentified flying object ferrying odd-looking passengers
overhead. Rumor has that it that a county sheriff spied a saucer-shaped
conveyance whirling above the local football field. He radioed the
sheriff's department and described something resembling a garden hose
dangling from the bottom of the saucer. The sheriff also claimed to have
received a terrific shock while viewing the extraterrestrial. He further
claimed the shock rendered him unconscious for a few minutes. When he
woke up, he witnessed the flying saucer trying to suck up electricity from
a nearby power plant. Apparently, electricity was required to run the
saucer's engine. It made quite a story, though it seemed to be missing a
few clarifying details, if you ask me.

Following that unusual interlude, Madam and I made our way
to Downsville Days, where I met two new friends, Bart and Bill. I
developed quite a fondness for draft horses and already had met quite
a few since coming to Minnesota. Bart and Bill spent most of their

days giving rides in a hay wagon or a sleigh, depending on the season. Today, it was a bunch of kids in a hay wagon enjoying the fun. The Downsville Days parade also included a bacon representative from El Paso and a flying saucer float sponsored by the Elm Wood Parks and Recreation Department.

Just down the road from Downsville, we met the Eleva Broiler Fest parade. Since we arrived late, Madam pulled over on the side of the road, so we could watch the procession pass. Meanwhile, the smoke from the chicken barbecue made it hard to see the floats. I did notice one fellow shooting cans of beer from something that looked like a bazooka. Apparently, Eleva had no firearm restrictions. Madam thought they had been celebrating for quite a while before we arrived. Even the Norwegian Pols and Springleik dancers looked a bit tipsy.

Our next stop involved cattle and a friend of Madam's who trains cow horses. "Cutting" refers to an event in which a cow horse and rider are judged on their ability to separate a single cow from a herd and keep it away for a short period of time. This was no small task. Ranchers like the McGarrys also used ranch cutting horses to help them capture and separate their cattle. A cutting horse operated like a large border collie—quick and to the point. This cattle management business was growing on me, though all I knew was what I learned at the McGarrys. That felt more like a cattle calamity than a cattle management program. A few days with the McGarrys, and Madam and I considered ourselves lucky to escape with our health and no blackleg vaccinations.

Today we were visiting a cowboy named Jasper Wright. A long driveway into the Wrights' place offered the first clue about how the visit might go. I could see from the Comfy Sundowner window that a small saddle in a nearby alfalfa field was about to collide with a hay baler. The baler slowly crawled through the windrows, gathering cut hay and compressing it into square bales. The farmer driving the tractor faced backward, enabling him to supervise the baling operation. He never noticed the saddle parked directly in his path. Well, you might guess the saddle lost that fight. The old baler didn't come out so well either. The farmer, who managed to avoid tumbling out of his tractor, shared a few choice words with anybody in hearing distance.

Though nobody from the Wright family witnessed this baling incident, the subject came up when Jasper asked his youngest son, Teddy, to saddle up his pony. That was about the time the neighbor showed up with something that looked like a quarter of beef with a lariat attached. He removed the object from the bed of his pickup and delivered it to the Wrights' front porch. By that time, Teddy had conveniently found himself a ride to a friend's house. His father stared silently at the ruined saddle before reaching for a cup of coffee and heading to the barn.

The whole Wright establishment resembled a ruined saddle. It consisted of a few sagging outbuildings and rusty gates swinging from their hinges. An outdoor arena built from scraps of wire and salvaged boards clung to occasional fence posts. This arrangement more or less kept the arena from falling down. Several well-used horses wandered about without any fences to prevent them from roaming the neighborhood. Others wearing saddles built from spare parts dozed in the driveway. Things were plenty relaxed. Nobody seemed to notice when a horse walked off the property. By now, the neighbors were probably accustomed to returning livestock and tack to the Wrights. Anyway, the horses seemed to appreciate the freedom.

As for Jasper, he was no sparkling beauty either. Unshaven and dressed in a faded North Dakota State sweatshirt, baggy jeans, and a dusty baseball cap, he stooped over the rear hoof of a young horse. After examining the hoof for a minute, he nailed on a recycled shoe designed for a bigger horse. Jasper practiced the economy plan when it came to his shoeing program. The same could be said when it came to his conversation. He subscribed to the theory that less was best. This being my first trip to the Wrights', I kept a close eye on Madam just in case she expected something from me. I could tell by the way Jasper looked me over that he thought I was too tall and probably knew nothing helpful.

Meanwhile, Madam was busy preparing to ride one of Jasper's horses. She certainly enjoyed having a go at working cattle. I kept my own counsel and watched while she swung one of Jasper's spare-parts saddles over an older-looking bay fellow named Dixie. She obviously knew this horse well—that meant she'd probably been slipping over here for months without telling me. Oh well, Dixie looked like a veteran, and I could use some pointers on cattle. I decided to slip down to the cutting pen and find a good viewing spot. They called it the cutting pen, but it looked more like a landfill project—something vaguely resembling a fence wrapped around scrub oaks and recycled posts.

Behind the fence, a three-legged picnic table rested against a stump, probably to prevent it from tipping. A Styrofoam cooler sat on top of the table. The cattle were doing their best to reach through the wire and grab the cooler. Hard to believe they planned to keep steers inside that Rube Goldberg contraption—two steers already had escaped. Just like Jasper's horses, they showed no interest in running away. The steers and I exchanged how-do-you-dos, and I retreated to a shady spot to watch.

Soon, Jasper came trotting down the path leading two extra horses, while Madam fiddled with her spare parts tack. She finally gave up and led Dixie into the pen, where she asked Jasper if he might have a bridle with both reins.

"Darn right," he replied, pointing to the saddle horn of one of his extra horses. No question; this was a man who avoided unnecessary chitchat.

By this time, three older Wright boys plus a neighbor girl showed up with their high school rodeo horses. They probably competed in a bunch of events, because the pen was littered with barrels and practice poles. The young people each had a rope, and it looked as if they planned to practice roping the overused steers.

Before anyone had a chance to get started, Jasper's dogs arrived—a lab mix named Sandy and a border collie named Rip. Rip looked competent and relaxed, by border collie standards. He took a seat on top of a barrel. Sandy, on the other hand, cavorted around the pen, randomly barking and nipping at any available heels. This brought a round of threats from the boys, though no amount of shouting influenced Sandy's conduct. Jasper finally started waving his hat and chased him out of the pen. Sandy continued to monitor events, though from outside the fence.

By this time, Madam had climbed aboard and was warming up Dixie. The bridle Jasper provided looked a little flimsy, but at least it had two reins. From what I could tell, old Dixie probably didn't care if he wore a bridle or went naked. He understood this routine and needed no coaching or fancy bits to get it done. Meanwhile, Jasper limped around, moving barrels out of the way, and then wrenched open a gate and shooed a half dozen steers into the cutting pen. Sandy continued loping around the outside. Rip sat motionless on his barrel, waiting for a cue. The steers took one look at this cast of characters and headed for the exit. My guess was they already had a bellyful of ropes, dogs, and cutting horses.

"Git a cow," barked Jasper at nobody in particular.

Madam looked at the rodeo crowd and concluded he was talking to her. She aimed Dixie at the steers, slipped around behind the herd, and cut one out from the rest. Until now, Dixie had struck me as a quiet horse, but his demeanor changed once he got in front of a cow. Well, actually, the steer swung around, eyeballed Dixie, and ripped off in Jasper's direction. Jasper must have said something insulting because the steer then dived back the other way, made a few sharp turns in each direction, and attempted to run under Dixie. Madam wisely said whoa to Dixie. Madam looked a little pale.

"Git another cow!" hollered Jasper.

She did. The second steer was agreeable enough to trot to the center of the pen and offer a few polite turns without trying to upend the horse. However, just about then, the oldest Wright boy ran his horse around the back of the herd and roped Madam's steer. "Just practicing!" he yelled with a grin. Again, Madam said whoa to Dixie.

"One more," barked Jasper, giving his son a look.

I hoped the third time would be the charm. Between the road-weary steers and the over-anxious cowboys, this show was headed in the wrong direction. Besides, old Dixie turned around so hard that he was digging holes in the dirt big enough to bury a suitcase.

Madam said nothing but returned to the herd a third time. She chose a quiet-looking steer that had been watching Sandy since he came into the pen. I was about to get my first lesson in which cattle to avoid. Dixie managed to move the steer away from the obsessing dog and away from his little herd of chums, but nobody expected the explosion that followed. Had this been a competition, the rider might have enjoyed a winning score. But this was not a competition, and Dixie continued to plow the ground as he clamped down, made hard turnarounds, and successfully stopped the steer. He countered each of the animal's moves with a tremendous effort that indicated he did not plan to lose this beast. The steer then bolted toward Jasper. Jasper shouted something rude. Dixie squatted and sprang hard to the left and then the right. At that point, Madam made one of those unplanned exits from the saddle.

It happened so quickly that she landed on her feet, holding the mismatched reins in one hand. Dixie slid to a stop. Madam took a little bow for both of them, thanking the audience for attending their little demonstration.

"Harrumph," muttered Jasper. "You need to fall off on your own darn time."

The cowboys took this as a cue that the cutting was done, and they could rope anything they could lay their lariats over. Hence, the pen became a high school rodeo dress rehearsal. The girl roped better than the three boys, but I didn't stick around to mention it.

Sandy continued to wear a path around the pen, ignoring everyone's shouts to quit. Rip stayed atop his barrel, and Jasper rode off over the hills, ponying the same two extras he'd brought from the barn.

Madam smiled and walked gingerly out of the pen, leading Dixie, who never really realized Madam had dismounted. Madam knew how sore she would be tomorrow. The day certainly offered plenty of excitement. Once again, I appreciated climbing back in the Comfy Sundowner and heading home to my own bed. As for a career in cutting, maybe moving a few lazy cows down the lane would be fun, but I'd leave the rest of it up to guys like Dixie.

21

I'm a Rock Star

Something was amiss at Evergreen. Since I'd arrived in
the spring, everyone had morphed into the same color—bay. I didn't
know how this happened. It was as if we'd turned into one big genetic
experiment that stopped at earth tones. Or worse, maybe we'd just
trended toward boring. In any case, a stroll down Evergreen's aisle
was now like a stroll through a row of corporate cubicles—dull and
repetitive. If memory served, our fabulous hodgepodge of shapes and
colors started to change when a bunch of Evergreen guests exited to
spend the summer in various lodgings and lake homes.

This began with the departure of two chestnuts and a buckskin
pony named Arrow. Soon, a second batch of black-and-dun ponies
packed up and took their leave for horse camp. Oh yes, a blond Belgian
with four white socks moved up to her partner's cottage for the summer.
Even the two paints signed up for ranch work in Wyoming, so they left

too.

About the same time, a laid-up racehorse named Skip the Champagne showed up (bay, of course). Next, we met the three Margaret Thatcher girls and a retired show jumper named Oleg—all bays. This didn't even cover Plum, Spruce, and Honey. Not an ounce of color, other than brown, on any of them. Now, every week brought a new brown face to Evergreen. As one who values diversity, I was puzzled by this change and hoped it didn't turn us into monotonous lumps.

Fortunately, Omar and Gabe remained with us. Their white coats provided the only spot of color—or lack thereof—as well as a perfect canvas for creative applications of mud and manure. The two constantly helped themselves to my fabulous silk shampoo and conditioner.

But this basic bay development really did worry some of us. Our dress code had become that of a humdrum marching band. These days, when Andres set out to collect someone from the pasture, he had to bring along registration papers that indicated any distinctive markings The farriers worried they might mistakenly shoe Oleg when they meant to give Bingo a pedicure. Yesterday the vet performed a flex test on a hunter named Sam—but he'd actually intended to examine a racehorse named Flyboy. A friend of Madam's became so confused last weekend that she rode a good-looking bay gelding in a dressage clinic. The problem was that the gelding belonged to someone else. For that matter, I could hardly tell myself from the other horses, which, of course was why I took good care of my luxurious mane and tail. If this kept up, we'd all have to wear ankle ID bracelets!

When Ms. Fendi, one of Evergreen's newer female guests, asked me what I did for a living and why I looked like everyone else, I was taken aback—make that slightly offended, especially since she too happens to be bay! For Pete's sake, I did *not* look like everyone else, nor did I *act* like anyone else. At least, I hoped not. Plus, what was it with these interviewers, poking their way into my personal life? First Ghillie tossed me a handful of probing queries. Then Ms. Fendi inquired about my professional intentions. She acted as if I should be announcing my candidacy for governor of Minnesota. I mean, who said we had to train for the Olympics to make the grade around here?

I happened to enjoy a little something new every day, not a steady diet of competition and professional upgrades. Truthfully, I wasn't quite making a living yet, not because I was lazy but because Madam made a living for the two of us. I provided the companionship and inspiration to help her to keep at it.

Anyhoo, I took a couple deep breaths and asked Ms. Fendi for a bit of clarification.

"I mean, what are you? A jumper, an eventer, a dressage contender? Do you ride to the hounds, or do you winter in Wellington, Florida?" she inquired with a superior tone.

"Well, not exactly," I said, stalling for time. "I'm an appendix quarter horse from Meeker, Oklahoma. Well, actually I'm now a Minnesota resident."

"And what is an appendix quarter horse?" she asked.

"Well, it's sort of a quarter horse hybrid. I'm actually an appendix quarter horse rock star," I explained, perhaps a bit too enthusiastically. "You might have read Dessa Hockley's book, *Is Your Horse a Rock Star?* According to her test, I'm just a confident, friendly, dazzling, all-round sort of guy. I love challenge and change. Lights! Camera! Action! I also have fans—even Facebook fans."

Ms. Fendi did not look terribly impressed. Then, she asked me what instrument an appendix quarter horse rock star played.

Oh, boy. "No instruments yet," I replied, "but I am considering the trombone," as if this might ignite some sign of approval from her. "Madam and I attend lots of parades with marching bands. I like the horns. And I'm learning to jump. I can jump almost anything if I feel like it. Oh yes, and I study Spanish. It helps my conversations with Andres and Jesus. They even tell me jokes in Spanish, just to check on my vocabulary."

Ms. Fendi looked doubtful. "Those don't sound like professions to me," she said, raising one eyebrow. "Those sound like hobbies. From what you tell me, you do nothing but play. You do know there is more to life than having fun, don't you?"

"Not really," I replied. "What's wrong with fun?" Then suddenly, I just couldn't help myself. "By the way, Ms. Fendi, I also like to trail cattle, write poetry, bake cookies, tour the country, play board games, and gallop in Baker Park. Oh, and you probably know I'm Evergreen Farm's chief entertainment officer."

If she remembered learning this detail on her arrival at Evergreen, she did not admit it. Maybe that was just too much information for her. On the other hand, she probably never met a guy with so many talents. Anyway, it felt good to say it out loud, especially the part about fun. She seemed awfully serious. Maybe I could teach her something about fun.

By this time I expected Ms. Fendi to turn on her hoof and march off in disgust. I was wrong.

"So, Noah Vail, do you do any of those things well?" she asked, gazing somewhat less imperiously down her elegant nose.

Good grief, why do I always get myself crosswise with girls like this? It was time to move our conversation in a new direction. "Why, yes," I said with my most dashing smile. "I bake a mean carrot cake. Would you care to join me for some tea and a little dessert?"

How could a girl resist?

22

The Goat Companion Question

All this late-summer heat meant that it was time for the
Minnesota state fair—my first time, no less! Our hot, dry weather also
caused the landlord to alter our bathing arrangements. We'd had to forgo
the indoor spa due to some plumbing mishap. Word was that some small
person had flushed an unseemly object down the hatch, causing the whole
works to choke. Now we had to wait for a plumber and do our cooling off
outdoors at the end of a garden hose. It wasn't as elegant as the spa, but I
found it every bit as refreshing. This, plus an industrial-size fan blowing
through my mane, and I was in heaven— not to mention clean.

Gabe complained bitterly but finally took a bath—an agreeable change, as he tends to slouch around in unwashed cribbage attire. But today he was traveling with me in the Comfy Sundowner, and it just seemed right that he tidy up. Besides, we hoped to march in the state fair parade, and I was sure the parade directors kept strict hygiene standards.

Fun-filled excitement or not, today brought a new dilemma. The state fair offered a blizzard of new vocational ideas, as if I needed any more confusion around that topic! Hardly a day passed that I didn't come up with a new job plan. For example, last weekend at the Scott County fair, we witnessed the most impressive draft horse competition—and I was obsessed with this exciting possibility. Those Belgian drafters cut quite a swath with their buff physiques and splendid harnesses. Plus, they managed to maneuver immense wagons around the exhibition area without even running down an announcer or tipping their drivers out in the dirt. (And the female members of these outfits served as the official team captains.) Ever since witnessing this, I'd been dreaming of a silver-studded harness and a red driving cart to haul around. How perfect would that be for all our local parades? It was very possible we could find just such treasures at the fair.

Madam loved the Minnesota state fair. Lately, she'd been chatting it up to anybody willing to listen. Just yesterday I heard her waxing nostalgic about her Eau Claire Trail Riders drill team that once competed at the state fair. Granted, this was a different time in history. A photo of her drill team suggested the girls must have designed their own costumes. About the only parts that matched were their red bandannas. I was amazed to hear that these youngsters camped overnight in the state fair horse barns. I was sure that today's child protection laws would prevent kids from planning slumber parties in a public horse barn. I guessed Gabe and I would find out soon.

I was sure we'd like the state fair, just as Madam did, especially the part where we'd make public appearances and sign autographs. This morning Gabe was to accompany me to the Moo Booth stage, where we'd get to watch them milk cows in front of the crowd. We also heard they'd give away peppermints just for spinning the moo-lette wheel, which we fully intended to do. Gabe also wanted to stop in at the Oink Booth. Madam said an oversized boar presided at that exhibit— make that the winner of the state's largest boar contest. Judging from his promotion poster, this boar's handlers made a colossal grocery investment in him. It was evident he knew nothing about moderation. I hoped he'd enjoy the company of horses, or Gabe and I might need to shorten our visit to the Oink Booth!

After that stop, we planned to tour the cattle barn and greet our friend Nettie's lovely Holstein heifers. That's when we'd call on a few goats. I still was shopping for a smallish goat companion, though the landlord did not care to promote any more goat ownership at Evergreen. Frankly, even I was having second thoughts about this idea. It seemed like such a good one when that stylish Olivia first paraded past my room with Bella in tow. However, Bella ate two of my good hats. She constantly was munching on peanuts and anything that came within eating distance of her room. She insisted that all goats craved peanuts. I really couldn't see myself running to the Costco to buy monster bags of peanuts for my little goat. Besides, I wondered if this would lead to peanut shells in my bed. It was an unresolved dilemma, and I was hoping today would shed new light on the subject.

Meanwhile, Gabe had agreed to help conduct more goat research as we toured the fairgrounds. He also was working on online research, a favorite pastime of his. Evergreen legend has it that he even hunted down cribbage CliffsNotes while browsing the Internet. Nobody has proof of this, but Gabe has not lost a game of cribbage in a very long time.

Madam appeared at 8:00 a.m. sharp to transport us to St. Paul for the day. I thought we should ask to march with one of those high school bands in the parade. We could get Madam to ask someone when we got there. The drive to the city took about an hour. Madam managed to find a convenient place to park next to a food concession shaped like a giant green pepper. It stood at the front door of the horse barn, a perfect place for us to begin. Actually, it previously stood there. Gabe read in the *Star Tribune* that the green pepper concession had suffered a head-on collision with some horses. Apparently, an ill-mannered team of

Clydesdales exited the barn on their own, taking out the green pepper as they made a sharp right-hand turn toward the coliseum.

That, however, was not the only morning eye-opener. We'd barely backed out of the Comfy Sundowner when a champion billy goat burst out of the sheep barn and leaped onto the hood of Madam's truck. Nobody knew how this dude had escaped, but he struck a majestic pose on the big Ram's hood. He looked as if he expected us to snap his photo. I suggested this might make a great picture for my website, but Madam disagreed. Once she dispatched the goat, she marched off in the direction of the barn manager's office. Gabe and I decided it was a good time to make our exit and head for the Miracle of Birth Barn.

There, we came upon a businesslike mother goat butting a veterinary student who was trying to deliver a lamb. Gabe says goats are especially fond of this kind of entertainment, most often during unguarded moments. Oh my, what might that mean for my enjoying an unguarded siesta in my own room? We were compiling more firsthand goat information than I'd expected.

After viewing the baby chicks, and a sow delivering twelve piglets, we left the Miracle of Birth Barn. That's when we came upon yet another goat. This one was nibbling on his owner's tennis shoes, as the young boy slept on a bale of straw. Oh dear, this did not bode well for the goat argument. Eating shoes, jumping on pickups, butting innocent bystanders—I'd never convince Madam that these activities were nothing more than a little goat fun. And my own zeal to find a goat companion was waning by the minute.

About then, Gabe and I decided we had witnessed enough miracles for the morning and changed our course. We toured the rabbit barn. We also admired some Belted Galloway cattle—they looked like Oreo cookies, with black outsides and lovely white stripes around the middle. When it came time for the parade, we zipped over to the grandstand and found a couple of empty places in front of a unicycle drill team. We decided to accompany the Iowa Old Abe's marching band. What a thrill to tramp side by side with the brass section. We figured this must be what a presidential inauguration felt like. Crowds waved from the curb, and firemen tossed Tootsie Rolls. Big horses pulled bigger wagons packed with political dignitaries, baseball players and, of course, Princess Kay of the Milky Way. It made a grand finale for the Great Minnesota Get-Together.

After the parade, Gabe and I thought we needed a caramel apple to top off the day. We had seen a lot without ever making it to the midway for a spin on the tilt-a-whirl. I admit that the whole goat-companion brainstorm lost its luster as the day progressed. Both Gabe and I concluded it would be best to wait a while before bringing home a goat. Surely Madam and the landlords would agree. Speaking of Madam, she was waiting for us at the Comfy Sundowner, armed with a bag of honey-dipped donuts. Once she straightened out the earlier goat incident with the barn manager, she and a couple of her friends had gone to watch the rodeo. That and a couple of corn dogs later made her day.

We concluded it was a fine day all around. By the time we hit Interstate 94, heading west, Gabe and I were drifting off to snoozeville, but two thoughts crossed my mind. I was relieved not to have to share my room with a goat that ate peanuts, and I really wanted to get good on the trombone.

23

Montana on My Mind

With the state fair behind us, Madam and I packed up for another adventure. This time we were aiming west to Montana to visit more ranching friends. We'd been invited to help round up cattle and drive them cross-country. I knew it was a long drive across North Dakota, but Madam had packed plenty of provisions, and we planned to make a few rest stops along the way.

Until now, my ranching experience had been limited to two visits to the McGarrys and one to Jasper Wright's place. Though we'd witnessed some Wild West events in both locations, Madam said

Montana stood alone when it came to cattle spreads. The McGarrys conducted a ranching business of much smaller proportions, and Jasper Wright used a freestyle approach to land and livestock management.

I didn't claim to be a perfect cow horse, but so far, I liked the vaquero life. It certainly beat some of the other uppity horse professions out there. Besides, I hoped to learn how to do more than herd Canada geese. I knew from reading *Western Horseman* magazine that this Montana escapade was going to give me a much better cow horse education than I'd had so far.

For starters, our hosts, the Harding family, managed their cattle on sixty thousand acres. Some of the land belonged to the family, and the rest belonged to the federal government—federal grazing land leased from the Bureau of Land Management. Given the size of this place, the first test involved finding the cattle. Once we found them, moving a large herd along the trail required experienced help, meaning cowboys and cowgirls who knew something about livestock. On this occasion, most of the help required some basic training. In fact, according to Madam, the trailer ride from Minnesota to Billings would feel like a Palm Springs vacation compared to the test I was about to face when we arrived at the Kinghorn Cross Ranch.

First, let me clarify a few details. One, I'm not fond of snakes. Not that I'd go out of my way to persecute snakes; I just wouldn't enjoy sharing my dinner or my bed with them. It's hard to like anyone whose conversation consists of a rattle. Madam, on the other hand, practically required CPR at the mention of snakes. For a woman who marched through life posing as courageous and self-assured, she wouldn't even make eye contact with the snake exhibit in the Department of Natural Resources building. Consequently, she would demonstrate no signs of reptile bravery on this trip. I would later learn that each night before bed, she scoured her bunkhouse, rifling through drawers and inspecting bathroom cabinets, hoping to find nothing but toilet paper. She also stopped drinking coffee. This might seem like a small detail, but anyone who drinks coffee knows it encourages rest stops. This requires short hikes through tall grass, and this was not going to happen. In fact, Madam refused to get out of the saddle, much less mosey through the sagebrush. She clearly planned to make my back her personal campsite for the next ten days.

Our roundup crew consisted of a mix of friends and neighbors with a broad range of ranching skills. And then there was a French woman with no experience beyond French food and fashion. We never figured out who invited her, as this promised to be a challenging assignment—and she had never ridden a horse. And while most of the crew wore work clothes—boots, protective chaps, and hats— she donned designer jeans that laced up her legs and showcased an enchanting amount of skin. Her fitted pants plus a pair of cherry-red Doc Marten boots and a peek-a-boo cowgirl shirt pretty much captured the hearts and minds of all the wranglers. As attractive a picture as this might paint, I made a note to keep my distance and let others look after any French emergencies that might arise on the trail.

On day one, the foreman, Big Mike, announced we would point west in search of a small bunch of rogue cattle that had escaped from a neighbor's pasture—not that we had any idea where these cows liked to hang out. Nobody even knew where the neighbors lived. Of course, that begged the question, what do we do with a bunch of snarky cows if we happen to stumble upon them? Well, no time for strategizing. Off we went, headlong into the land of snakes and varmints. Within a mile or so, a cowboy named Clint suggested that Madam and I take a jaunt up the side of a steep bluff to see what we could find on top. We started our climb up the rocky trail. The trail then morphed into a slim footpath, which then disappeared altogether. It was not until we reached the very top that I realized our friendly trail featured steep cliffs on both sides.

I must make a small confession here. Neither Madam nor I appreciated heights. Yet the day had hardly begun, and we already had scaled some kind of mountain with no sign of cattle or a safe way down. Now, the Midwest offers precious few cliffs on which to practice, and our scenic route was starting to make me nervous. About this time, Madam interrupted my trance by suggesting we keep moving forward. *Okey dokey*, I agreed, since no other good ideas came to mind.

Much to my amazement, we came face-to-face with a handful of black cattle. This small though unfriendly looking herd gawked at us in disbelief. They had to wonder how a mature woman, riding an

inexperienced, very tall horse, managed to hunt them down. I thought it
was a real triumph on our part. No need to tell the rest of group we
practically swooned over the altitude. In any case, we had no time to
waste. These motley cattle looked to be dreaming up an escape. I eased
my way around the back of the herd, hoping to point them in the general
direction we wanted to move. Unfortunately, they viewed my nudging as
an insult. Instead, they took off as if we had tossed a cherry bomb. Me oh
my, they headed straight for the cliff at a wide-open run. I quickly
followed. The goal here was to avoid taking a swan dive over the edge of
the cliff while arriving safely at the bottom of the bluff.

Well, one thing led to another, and thankfully, Madam kept quiet
while I mulled over our options. At one point, I heard some sunbathing
snakes beneath my feet, rattling as we galloped overhead. We were
quickly closing in on decision time, but the cattle showed no sign of
slowing. Picture our alarm when the whole herd suddenly disappeared
from view. Had they shot off the cliff like a bovine rocket? Or fallen into
a colossal hole? Heavens no! They sailed right over the edge, leaving
behind a dust explosion too thick to see through. Down they skidded,
wallowing through the steep terrain. We quickly abandoned plans of
gently nudging these critters toward home. Instead, Madam and I joined
them on their descent. This plunge of ours broke a cow-herding speed
record. Not that much herding was going on. This was more like
skydiving in sagebrush. Yet I'm glad to report that everyone made it to
the bottom more or less intact, though wheezing and filthy. Note to
Madam: Montana cattle do not act like docile dairy cows.

Meanwhile, Madam's friend Dave, who had nodded off while
waiting for us, looked up just in time to witness a mountain of dirt and
four-legged beasts coming his way. Dave, a soft-spoken city slicker,
prefers a quiet cattle drive. Our approach did not qualify as quiet.
Furthermore, soft-spoken Dave had singlehandedly gathered a large herd
of cattle while we were touring the cliff district. Who knew from whence
this bunch of cattle came? Like Dave, his newly acquired herd was
enjoying a little catnap—that was, until we came into view. By the time
Madam and I reached Dave, the two herds had exchanged hellos and
headed off toward Billings at a dazzling rate of speed. At this point, we
were pretty much on our own. Cattle gone, and our fearless crew

members probably back at the ranch enjoying a hot breakfast.

We soon learned that the rest of the crew had not gone straight home but were lollygagging along the path in front of us. We could have used some help, but I'm sure I heard some woman singing camp songs. This did not sound like help to me. I was beginning to wonder how Big Mike found such a pitiful group of ranch hands. Madam expressed similar thoughts, though with words I'd never heard her use. Even the wranglers had disappeared. Or perhaps they chose to supervise the French woman in the lace-up pants. In any case, the four of us, including Dave's horse, Smitty, gave up trying to head off the stampede. Instead, we stayed as close as possible behind the herd. Eventually, an irritable old cow changed up the plan. She took a sharp right up a draw and into a swamp. The rest of her minions followed, as did we.

The only good thing about this detour was our pace slowed considerably. This gave Dave and Madam a few minutes to review the morning's activities thus far. Between the Olympic hill climb and the stampede, nobody even checked to see whose cattle we'd apprehended. The trick now was to get them back to the ranch, where the lollygaggers could do the sorting and return them to their rightful owners. The cattle, for their part, managed to wallow through the mud and jam themselves up against a fence. A handful of mother cows eyed us from the other side of the fence. Fortunately, they made no attempt to join our herd. It took us a good hour and some serious bellowing to extract our renegades from the muck and turn them toward ranch headquarters.

Luckily, all this charging up and down mountains took the edge off everyone, including the cows. This made, the rest of the return trip to the ranch pretty quiet, just the way Dave liked it. When Big Mike finally saw us coming, he swung the gate open to make room for our prize. The weary herd ambled through the gate and buried their faces in a pile of hay and a tank of water. At least we all got a little rest until after lunch.

Actually, "after lunch" came far too soon. Madam and I happily left the cattle sorting to a couple of ranch hands, while the rest of us saddled up and got ready to trail the merged herds of cattle back to the neighbor's. Up the lane we went for a mile or two before someone mentioned it would be a ten-mile trip each way. So off we shambled, trailing somebody's ill-tempered cattle somewhere. After this morning's jaunt, Madam wisely chose not to volunteer our services for anything. We left all serious cow-hunting up to the experts—or at least to the others. Meanwhile, the French woman looked rested and tidy in her stylish jeans. Could she have stayed home all morning? The cowboys continued to hover around her like a bunch of tour guides.

The cattle behaved better after lunch than they had in the morning. They processed at a mere plod, in comparison to the earlier charge of the dust brigade. Consequently, the wranglers decided to stir up some entertainment for the rest of us. Madam worried that their entertainment might include rattlesnakes, such as it had the day before. We both voted for less showbiz, though somebody quickly voted us down.

Sure enough, Cowboy Clint stepped off his horse and challenged the lead cow to a footrace. This did not strike me as a good idea. Young Clint would have been smart to challenge Mrs. Angus from atop his horse, rather than from eye level on the ground. Once he hit the dirt, she took him at his word, and the chase began. Clint made a couple of revolutions around the herd, whooping it up, with Mrs. Angus closing the gap behind him. Once Clint noticed the cow gaining on him, he made a quick turn into the middle of the herd. This created quite a disturbance. Cattle dispersed in all directions, wringing their tails and bawling with disapproval. From that point on, any plans of quietly moving cows were out of play.

I failed to mention that the Kinghorn Cross Ranch also raised good quarter horses. Since they own several breeding stallions, each one enjoys his personal band of mares. For the most part, this herd method runs smoothly. Problems arise only when a couple of groups bump into one another, or a stallion gets testy about his territory and personal possessions. Apparently, today was the day for this kind of encounter. We no sooner spotted one of the ranch stallions and his ladies than a second stallion appeared. The second one, however, came from a nearby wild horse sanctuary (underscore "wild"). By the way, wild horses know nothing about diplomacy.

The term "perfect storm," while mostly overused, applied to

this new situation. I could see three developing problems: one cowboy on the ground; a few dozen narrow-minded cattle dispersing faster than an oil spill; and two stallions preparing to discuss their females. As for the first problem, Clint quickly managed to get back on his horse. The cattle eventually slowed to a lope, finally becoming bored with the whole enterprise. Meanwhile, the stallions' meet-and-greet took a downright dangerous turn. The wild horse eyeballed every moving thing, sizing us up as either threat or possible acquisition. Madam had begun to plan our getaway when Big Mike suddenly cracked a bullwhip and shouted, "*Run!*" Nobody waited for more details.

Oh boy, another stampede, barring Clint and a wrangler who stayed behind to chase the wild horses off. Some ran away, while others tried to follow the ranch stallion. The wild stallion circled the ranch mares, intending to pick off a few to take with him. Fortunately, the cattle gave up running and wringing their tails and went to grazing.

If I understand anything well, it's running. Madam and I led the charge as we raced through a stand of trees and thorny underbrush. I could hear shrieks and crashing sounds coming from behind, but none sounded life threatening, so we kept up the pace for about a mile. It wasn't until we pulled up on top of a small rise that I saw something was amiss with the French woman. She hung back from the rest of the group, unwilling or unable to join us. Meanwhile, Big Mike took a quick head count while everyone gasped for air. Miraculously, the entire party escaped the stallions' dust-up without getting trampled—well, except for the French woman. At first, we thought one of the stallions might have kicked or bitten her. But no, that was not the case. Though she managed to stay on her horse through the ordeal, the getaway through the heavy brush made quick work of her lace-up designer jeans. She now wore nothing more than French lace underpants with her Doc Marten boots.

I'm sure this marked a first for all the cowboys. Nobody at the Kinghorn Cross Ranch had ever lost his or her pants while trailing cattle. Actually, it seemed an impossible feat. Pant removal requires stepping out of each leg, a difficult maneuver on solid ground, not to mention in a saddle at a gallop. Obviously, this clothing malfunction caused quite a to-do among the wranglers. Nobody quite knew how to proceed, and nobody felt like approaching the woman to discuss her dilemma. She was, I might mention, wearing very attractive lingerie. Finally, Clint and the rest of the boys showed up. After a brief consult with Clint, Big Mike came up with a plan. He removed his chaps and hung them over a branch. He then requested we all move down the trail and give the French woman a little privacy while she slipped into the chaps. Sometimes a creative solution trumps a perfect one!

At this point, the cattle-moving enterprise came to an end for the day. Between the wild horse standoff and the vanishing designer pants, everyone felt like calling it quits. We left the cattle project for the next day and moved off in the direction of dinner—at least, that's what Big Mike said we were doing. We learned later that a couple of the cowboys returned the cattle to the neighbors without our help, a wise choice on their part.

The walk back to the lodge gave Madam and me time to discuss the Kinghorn Cross Ranch experience thus far. We concluded that the day's assignment exceeded our capacity for excitement. She also reminded me that our Montana trip just had started. We had a week to go before returning to the safety of Evergreen Farm. I couldn't help wondering what else could happen to rival this. It would be pretty hard to top a French woman hurtling through the woods, pursued by a wild stallion, and dressed only in pink lace undies and Doc Marten boots. I couldn't wait for tomorrow.

24

It's All Part of a Horse's Job

I didn't know if it was some kind of seasonal disorder, or if Madam just thought I was stinky from our long road trip to Montana, but she and Mrs. Landlord suddenly were inspired to break out the soap and trash bags and plug in the Hoover upright. The landlord calls it fall house cleaning. Or maybe she'd said fall *horse* cleaning. In any case, Evergreen looked like a Merry Maids convention, and I could see that I was going to be next in line to get a good scrubbing. True, I might have picked up a few ticks and fleas from bunking with all those dusty ranch horses, but this obsession with tidiness had become rather annoying.

And that wasn't all. Madam's tack trunk mysteriously appeared at my door. She referred to it as *our* tack trunk, though its contents really had very little to do with me. Evergreen's barn cat Fang spent more time in that darn box than anyone, which might explain the peculiar fragrance wafting my way. The only time I saw the tack trunk's contents was when Madam emptied it in a musty pile in front of my room. With that, she'd look expectantly in my direction, as if I should know how to take inventory or properly dispose of this stuff. Well, if you want my opinion, the whole mess looked like it belonged in the trash.

Nothing appeared any too fresh, that's for sure. We had the odd-looking pink lumps she tried to pass off as horse treats. I believe those were a birthday gift from last February. They could be petrified or even poisonous by now. I also saw a pair of muck boots, actually more muck than boots. Then there was one leather glove, minus the pinky finger, no doubt consumed by a mouse. And what about that can of Stickum Behinder Glue? That was the stuff that kept her behinder stuck in the saddle when we rode in the park. It also worked when we practiced my flying lead changes.

"You had better not lose that stuff," I chuckled with a wink and a snort.

"Not funny," replied Madam.

Oh dear, I could see she was not in tip-top humor. And lookie here—a furry bundle of something took up residence in the bottom of her running shoe at the bottom of the trunk. It was hard to say—this could be animal or vegetable—so I suggested to Madam that she might want to slip on a pair of rubber gloves or try the vacuum. Well, well, I did see something of mine after all—a bag of my exceptional, natural silk hair-care products. The bottles looked as if she'd been storing them in a compost pile. They were covered in grime and probably had been fair game to every mouse and pigeon in Hennepin County.

And then I saw dust billowing out the tack room door. I didn't really think tack rooms needed a vacuum treatment, but there was no stopping these women at that point. The landlord posted firm instructions about how to reorganize everything. So many new guests had arrived, and they'd brought way too many personal belongings with them.

The landlord was striding my way carrying something that looked familiar—my bridle for goodness sake! She asked, ever so politely, if I could find a new place to hang it, as the tack room now was full.

"Well, not really," I said, glancing around my room, looking for any extra hooks. "Don't our bridles belong in the tack room?" She scowled. I checked the clock, hoping Andres would show up to rescue me from this torturous cleaning frenzy.

That's when things took an even more challenging turn. Madam came sauntering down the aisle, chewing on a list of complaints as long as my Buck Brannaman lead rope. She began with last night's annoying back pain that led to insomnia, which then turned into anxiety over her work. This forced her to get out of bed at 4:00 a.m. and bake something. That evidently did not go well, judging from the lopsided coffee cake she just slipped into Evergreen's lunchroom.

I listened, courteously nodding in agreement, while she unwound a string of protests. It was an inclusive list—the high price of produce to the neighbor who criticized her ugly garden shed. (The shed, incidentally, should have been condemned by a public health agency.) Next, she started in on the new hair color that made her look like her great-aunt Maude, the one with long earlobes and pink hair. After that, it was a rant about the stock market and her underwhelming retirement plan, plus the need to replace her washer and dryer, both so old they carried the discontinued Lady Kenmore label. It was downright exhausting to listen to her, but I remained attentive to a fault.

"And why is it that perfectly capable children vanish when it's time to rake and put the garden to bed?" she further queried, without waiting for an answer from me.

"I don't know," I offered carefully. Perhaps it was because they lived in a condo 250 miles away and didn't own a rake—I only thought this but did not mention it. I could easily see this was not the time or place for making such observations.

"And wouldn't I just love to have one of those mid-life crises that includes travel to exotic parts of the world, eating and loving, and thinking grand thoughts?" she continued and then huffed, "Who the heck can afford those kinds of trips anyway?"

If I remembered the number of candles on her last birthday cake correctly, she was using the term "mid-life crisis" rather loosely. Besides, a woman could have a perfectly fine mid-life crisis right here at home, as long as she had a strong and handsome horse at her side to help her through the rough patches. Madam and I already had discussed this part of my job description.

There I was, on a lovely fall morning, held captive by Madam's mutterings—and soon, the dreaded vacuum. Some days, it felt like my role changed 180 degrees, from attractive, multitalented equine professional to that of a lowly husband or bartender or even a hairdresser. Yet Madam thanked me kindly for my wise counsel. In this case, as in many cases with friends and relatives, the wisest counsel amounted to *no* counsel.

25

When to Say No to Gardening

I never had a yen to garden. This was a rare thing, as nearly everything interested me. But I did have my reasons for shunning the seed and the sprinkler business. In the first place, horses find it challenging to operate spades and trowels. I have enough trouble trying to type a simple e-mail. Digging holes in the dirt with a shovel simply did not ring my proverbial bell. Second, why would I pay for compost to be delivered when Andres helped me remove it from my room every day? It simply was a practical observation worth mentioning.

Madam, on the other hand, nearly would swoon when the first seed catalog arrived in her mailbox. Tulips, lilies, lilac bushes, or green beans—she was a fan of every growing thing. She even had a Burpee clock in her kitchen that must have been manufactured in about 1876, when the seed company was founded. Theoretically, the clock displayed helpful facts about when to plant and when phases of the sun and moon occur. It was sort of like an Old Farmer's Almanac that happened to tell time. By the way, her enthusiasm for growing plants and veggies far surpassed her aptitude for gardening, though that never served as a deterrent.

A case in point: this past spring, about the time of my arrival at Evergreen, she decided to expand her petite kitchen garden into a plot suitable for an entire community. The first step required a neighbor with a John Deere tractor to break up the soil with a disk. Then she hired a guy from a local tree farm to deliver a pickup truck full of composted something or another. Thus, that little sharecropper's heaven of hers started to look like Untiedt's Produce Farm in Waverly, Minnesota, that magnificent spread that cultivates everything from rhubarb and raspberries to sweet corn, squash, tomatoes, and most any other fruit and vegetable that can survive a Minnesota winter.

Size, however, did not necessarily spell success with the gardening enterprise. Madam planted everything from potatoes to broccoli. Sweet corn occupied one corner, while tea roses flourished in another. Carrots, tomatoes, and lettuce covered a large portion of her front yard. While this might sound like a stunning triumph, everything grew to impossible sizes. The sweet corn towered over her, making it impossible to reach the ears. Potatoes masquerading as shrubbery threatened to take over the front porch. Giant heads of cauliflower created a sensation when she realized they served as home to a large white worm population. Unfortunately, nobody noticed this until Madam popped the cauliflower heads into boiling water and all the worms jumped out. That ended the blanch-and-freeze operation. After that, even the cat shunned the garden, for fear of being consumed by hulking broccoli ... or perhaps a white worm. Actually, none of the pets went near the garden. Everything grew so tall, it cast long shadows, making a simple walk through the cosmos feel like visit to an Alfred Hitchcock movie set.

All this said nothing of the weeds! They too stood tall and robust. Clearly, the truckload of compost did its magic. Swedish saws and hatchets quickly replaced spades and grass clippers. Weed management became a full-time job. Lack of weed management resulted in the disappearance of an entire crop of radishes. Actually,

Madam lost the weed management challenge way back in July. It was frightening, even to a brave horse such as I.

By the end of the growing season, Madam faced a predicament: should she continue whacking things down with a two-woman saw, or should she invite the neighbors over to pick at their own risk? She finally decided to throw a party, and go for a farmer's market theme. She invited friends and neighbors, though she warned them of the dangers of rotator cuff injuries. That's when Omar and the boys joined me for a little garden tour of our own. We jumped in the Comfy Sundowner and asked the landlord to drive us to Madam's urban produce plot. We then took a wheelbarrow and gathered an abundance of fruits and veggies for our own use. After some serious picking, we headed back to Evergreen. It was time to send invitations to our very own harvest party, complete with hayrides and apple bobbing. Madam might not make it as a master gardener, but she surely knew how to produce some great ingredients for a party!

26

A North Woods Encounter

Every now and again Madam got an itch to drive north to the Boundary Waters Canoe Area. She really enjoyed the Gunflint Trail, which happened to be home to the Gunflint Lodge, a fave for all of us. It also was home to some new equine friends, plus a hodge-podge of wild creatures I'd never met in my former home of Oklahoma. Plus, the holidays were approaching, and a lot of good food was served at the Gunflint Lodge on Thanksgiving day. Even equine guests enjoyed a special holiday menu.

I had no intention of getting left behind, so I lassoed Mrs.

Landlord and asked if she would loan me her Hoover upright to spiff up the Comfy Sundowner. Gabe and I had left it in a state, following our last outing to the Minnetonka Orchard. "Too much cribbage and not enough hygiene," the landlord proclaimed after surveying the wreckage. She was right; it definitely needed a deep cleaning, and I figured Merry Maids didn't do horse trailers.

Once Gabe and I got things shipshape, I invited Omar to join me for the holiday weekend. The two of us had such a fine time on our last Gunflint expedition, it seemed only right to include him in a Thanksgiving jaunt. One thing about Omar—he was fun to travel with, because he rarely whined about anything. And another thing, unlike the landlord, he hardly ever said I talked too much. Plus, he definitely appreciated a good menu. Of course, we wouldn't be traveling alone this time. Madam reported that two of her book-club chums and three hairball pets would be joining us. She means well when she invites friends and beasties to take part in our road trips, but she and I sometimes need our quiet time together—a peaceful drive, a cozy cabin, and space to reflect on the meaning of Thanksgiving. Oh well, at least Omar and I had reserved our own cabin. The last trip north found us in charge of Madam's elderly Jack Russell and the Fluff Muffin Cat—that task was not without its challenges.

Departure day arrived, and I was trying to help pack. It was one thing to motor down the road with just Omar and me tucked in the Comfy Sundowner—we didn't require much more than a few groceries and level-headed driver. It was quite a different matter to pack up the hairballs and a young poodle that didn't rest much. This trio and three adult females could have used a UPS truck to transport their load. According to my checklist, that load included one pony-sized folding kennel, two large dog beds, two pet watering gizmos, doggie outerwear, doggie underwear, and doggie kibble. Then I saw a second pile of goods. The number two pile included a large cooler, parkas, suitcases, snacks, magazines, overshoes, and a kitty litter box—and the cat was not shy about using said kitty litter box while in transit. This might sound like a dandy convenience for the cat, but it forced passengers to open the windows wide and let in a good dose of bracing air.

Another challenge: Madam's two hairball pets really should

have been living at the Mayo Clinic, for all the prescriptions and special health food they required. In addition to their culinary and medical needs, they also required constant supervision. At any moment, either of them could wander off to play canasta with total strangers. Worse yet, they might get mistaken for gray-wolf hors d'oeuvres.

Given all the baggage we attempted to stuff in the car, I'd be shocked if we didn't get stopped by the highway patrol and ticketed for reckless packing. But the packing was done, and we finally were launched. The drive up Interstate 35W through Duluth and up Highway 61 past Betty's Pie Shop went smoothly enough. It was the rest stop that got complicated. Everyone needed a rest room. The book club group wasted no time exiting the vehicle, but while they dawdled over which jackets to wear and where to put their coffee cups, the cat slipped out. He quickly took off on a self-directed tour of the grounds. The poodle then started a row with a Labrador tied to a pickup truck next door. All the while, the women lingered in the restroom, the elderly Jack Russell barked at each dog and human that came too close to the car. Oh my, we had four hours of travel before we'd reach our destination.

Two rest stops and one poodle barf later, we were motoring along the Gunflint Trail, hoping we hadn't missed dinner. We also hoped not to encounter a moose in the road. I'd never seen a moose but understood they weren't compatible with motorized vehicles. Fortunately, the pets snoozed for part of the way. For the other part, the elderly Jack Russell ran laps from one seat to the other. Omar and I witnessed this through our window, with deep appreciation for our separate seating arrangements.

Once we arrived, Omar and I took our leave from the rest of the crew and hiked up the hill to our lodging—a residence next door to the Gunflint stable. This ideal setup gave us an excellent view of Madam's cabin, as well as a break from the barking dogs. Even good-natured Omar asked if I'd packed anything for a headache. Ah, but the food looked delicious, and the weather was crisp, with just a dusting of snow on the ground. Maybe after dinner, we all could sign up for wolf calling.

We could see that the book ladies managed to get a fire going and unpack. They also must have sampled a bit of liquid refreshment before dinner, because we could hear a good deal more laughter than we'd heard on the drive up. Actually, I could hear more laughter from them than from any cabin around us. Omar and I began to wonder if they had invited guests in, but that seemed unlikely, as we'd just arrived.

Then the door opened, and the dogs shot out to find their own restroom. The poodle promptly took off after a deer, and the elderly Jack Russell cornered a chipmunk in the cabin vestibule. This did not look like a good thing. No surprise that shouting ensued. Finally, Madam and the poodle's boss, Monica, wrestled the two dogs back into the cabin. The chipmunk bolted around the vestibule a time or two and then escaped. We could hear screams all around. The three women finally managed to get themselves out the door and off to sample a plate of walleye and perhaps another glass of wine.

This was exactly the way things went—a little walleye and a little chardonnay. Two hours later, as Omar and I were nodding off to snoozeville, I heard singing. It sounded like another camp song serenade, though this one was parading our way. *The neighbors will love this*, I thought. Then, there was silence, followed by muffled, distinctly female voices.

"Whew," I whispered to Omar, who looked stumped.

"Whew, what?" he croaked with a shiver.

"It's just the book club rehearsing a few tunes," I reassured him. "Book tunes?" he queried. "Book tunes in the woods? In the dark?"

"Well, something like that," I replied in my most comforting tone.

Drat. Another eerie sound drifted out of the night and into our window—not singing this time. It sounded more like moaning. *Yip yip ahwoo. Yip yip ahwoo.* Good grief, the book club girls must have been trying to converse with a wolf. The lodge naturalist might not appreciate this. Another welcomed silence followed the ahwooing. Then, someone or something answered. Omar's teeth started to chatter. *That was definitely a wolf*, I concluded, though I did not share that information with Omar. That second glass of wine must have boosted the women's wolf-courting confidence, because soon enough, they resumed their ahwooing, in spite of the neighbor's protests.

By now, the elderly Jack Russell and the poodle had tuned up their own vocal chords. A couple in the neighboring cabin shouted out the window that they would prefer if everyone stopped speaking wolf. Actually, they weren't quite that polite. I could hear female giggling bubbling up through the dark. It was at that point that I made an executive decision not intervene unless somebody started throwing rocks or tomatoes. Holy cow, we'd been here less than three hours, and some kind of forest fracas already was breaking out.

Adding to the developing scene, Omar now was fully awake and convinced that wolves were about to break down our door. The howling threesome then quit howling long enough to make it to their cabin without meeting the neighbors. I did, however, have a feeling the lodge management would be hearing about this. It took me two hours and three gin rummy games to get Omar back to sleep.

The next morning after breakfast, I suggested to Madam that we might want to do something quiet and relaxing that did not involve neighbors or wolves. She looked a little sheepish but agreed to a hike with John, the naturalist. We all set out to Magnetic Rock. On the way, we met a fisher, a weasel wearing snazzy fur. We also visited the Chik-Wauk Museum, where John gave us an impressive history lesson on the Gunflint's prehistoric beginnings. By lunchtime, Omar was starting to get in the groove and enjoy himself. After lunch, we met a pileated woodpecker, a barred owl, and a large gathering of deer—all girls, I might add. They seemed rather sociable for wilderness deer, though they might have thought Omar and I looked like dating material.

Just as we started hiking back to the lodge, the stable boss, Marla, showed up to say she wanted us to meet her newest hire, Bart. The stable was only a short walk past the sled dogs that had just arrived for the winter. We did wonder why Bart was still here—Gunflint horses usually left by Thanksgiving and returned in May. *Oh well, there must be a good explanation*, I thought. So we trotted on down the road to the stable.

What a surprise! Our first thought was that Bart looked like something from the Chik-Wauk Museum's collection of prehistoric beginnings. We decided he must be some special breed of North Woods draft horse—a horse with a rather irregular looking nose. He wore a large hat, which we later learned was not a hat at all but a pair of specialty antlers. On top of that, he towered over all of us. He even made Omar look like a Shetland pony. I felt somewhat weak in the knees at the sight of him. And poor Omar suffered another onset of teeth chattering.

Marla must have seen our surprised expressions, because she quickly explained that Bart was not a horse at all. He was a moose. He helped them work in the woods, hauling lumber and other large items.

Large items indeed! A moose? Well, that took the cake. As I said, I'd never met a moose, but this Bart looked quite different from what I'd expected.

"I didn't know moose wore horse clothing and worked for a living," I squeaked.

"Ah, but this one does," replied Marla. "He's quite a special moose."

Yes, I can see that, but special in what way? I wondered. *That's certainly a specially made harness he's wearing. And he has his own wagon the size of a Greyhound bus. Boy, those big Clydesdales at the Scott County fair could use a guy this big on their team.*

"But, aren't moose slightly temperamental?" I whispered to Marla.

"That depends," she replied.

"Depends on what? Depends on which side of the bed he got up?" I chuckled, attempting a little moose humor. Marla didn't catch the humor.

"It depends on how well you treat him," she said. "You might notice, he looks different from you do, and he's had some difficulties fitting in with the horses. This is why I'm going to rely on you and Omar to smooth the path for him when the others return in the spring. You'll have to come back for Memorial Day weekend and help make sure they treat him kindly and include him in their games."

Good heavens, in one year, I'd undergone a transformation from a racehorse to a life coach for a moose. This did not strike me as an upwardly mobile career move. I pondered how in the world we might approach this assignment.

Omar, who listened to the entire conversation from a safe spot behind the book club ladies, suddenly stepped up and actually said something. "How about inviting him over for some gin rummy and a bucket of popcorn?"

It was a bold proposal for a guy whose teeth had been chattering for the past twelve hours but a fine idea and worth a try!

"Ah, Bart, can we interest you a little card game this evening?" I asked.

He simply nodded agreeably and said he would be there at 7:00 p.m. sharp.

The word sharp gave me pause, but soon we learned that Bart was a detailed sort of moose. Not only did he arrive at 7:00 sharp, he played a sharp game of gin rummy. He also asked if we would like to learn about orienteering. Omar and I looked at one another blankly. Bart then explained that orienteering was a land navigation sport he practiced up here in the woods. Kind of like a treasure hunt with a compass and a funky map. The lodge was sponsoring an orienteering contest the next morning, and he invited us to join his team.

"Yes, of course, we would love to," I declared. When it came time for Bart to go home, we agreed to meet the next morning at 8:00.

It snowed silently during the night. Early the next morning, everyone gathered at the lakefront to get instructions for the competition. We all got maps with instructions and a scorecard. Omar and I knew nothing about orienteering, so we spent the morning trotting from one checkpoint to another, following Bart, who obviously knew his way around a map and a compass. We passed the lodge and waved at Madam and her friends, lingering over breakfast. Then we trotted up the hill past the stable and around the sled dog kennels. We even galloped for a stretch—a big surprise to see a moose gallop! When it was all over, we had made it to the finish point first. We'd actually won! Well, Bart won. His prize was a black leather bell collar with some added bling for the upcoming holiday season. Omar and I won a large basket of Haralson apples, our very favorite.

We were sad to pack up and say good-bye to Bart but promised we would see him again in the spring when the horses returned. He agreed that sounded like a good plan. For a guy who scared the stuffing out of us twenty-four hours ago, he'd turned out to be the highlight of the Gunflint Thanksgiving trip. Well, Madam and the book ladies, with their wolf-calling caper, also provided some good entertainment. Yet Omar and I decided Bart won the prize. Maybe my transformation from racehorse to life coach had more possibilities than I'd thought.

27
Kitty Mysteries

I'd like to report a conversation I had with Madam's
number two hairball pet—the cat. To be more specific, the Fluff Muffin
Cat, Mickey, who toured around Minnesota like the dog, perched on the
console of Madam's Subaru Outback; the cat that nonchalantly goes poo-
poo in his kitty box while Madam tries to keep the car on the road. Well,
this morning, in the spirit of the approaching holiday season, I asked the
Fluff Muffin if he might like my help writing a letter to Santa—or to
whomever cats commune at holiday time. The Fluff Muffin gave me the
cat *look*. Unlike the Jack Russell *look*, which typically involves food or
rodents, this one implied I could use coaching in feline political
correctness. It did not qualify as a warm-fuzzy look.

As much as I enjoy all creatures, great and small, my knowledge
of kitty culture appeared to be wanting. My choice of small talk fell flat,
so I finally asked him about his health. He rolled his eyes. Incidentally,

this cat did not meow. He chirped—and rather girly chirps at that. I did understand a little Spanish, but I didn't understand feline chirps coming from the mouth of a robust male cat. As I seemed to be getting nowhere, I decided to try a few interview questions—the leading kind of questions that sometimes catch a cat off his guard.

"What do cats like for Christmas or Hanukkah—or birthdays, for that matter?" I inquired.

"Nothing," he chirped rather dismissively.

"Surely you must want something," I persisted. "Maybe you could use a new hat or a game of kitty Monopoly? How about your very own fishbowl? Perhaps you'd like an iPod or a mouse soufflé?" He missed the humor in that one, of course.

Silence. Then he chirped, "I like my box."

"Does that mean you want a new box?" I queried.

"No, I like this one. And tell Santa or the UPS person who oversees box deliveries not to launder or vacuum my box either," he instructed firmly. "Actually, I wish you would give Madam that same message. Just when I get the hair and toys perfectly arranged in my current box, she tosses the whole works into the washer. Then I have to start all over, organizing fragrances and what not."

"I know what you mean," I offered. "She does have this cleanliness obsession."

On one hand, it certainly would simplify Madam's holiday gift list if she only had to provide the Fluff Muffin with a new box or keep her hands off his current box. On the other hand, I'd never met anyone who didn't want some special gift, especially at the holiday.

"No flat screen TV? No trip to Barbados?" I persisted.

Mr. Fluff had hardly changed position in that box since the last time I photographed him. That was in September, for my Facebook fan page. It was a kitty mystery if I'd ever seen one.

Coincidently, the next morning, while delivering my holiday cookies at Evergreen, I discovered Snuggles snoozing in a similar cardboard box. (Incidentally, this box was designed for a much smaller cat than Snuggles.) I actually mistook her for a coonskin hat lodged in an Ariat purse, though I did not share this observation with her.

As I pondered this new box situation, it made me wonder if

this was another one of those cat-in-the-box eccentricities practiced by the Fluff Muffin. Perhaps, but unlike Madam's city kitty, Snuggles was a proper barn cat. She was an upstanding hunter, a savvy prowler, and a girl who liked to mix it up with the neighborhood roughnecks. Snuggles actually could scale a vertical wall and make it to the haymow when in pursuit of a chipmunk. Somehow, it struck me as odd that she suffered from the same cat-in-the-box malady as the Fluff Muffin. Hence, I asked Snuggles how she liked her Costco box.

"I love it," she replied, with a long, leisurely stretch.

"And tell me, have you had a chance to post any holiday gift requests?" I asked.

"Why, yes," she purred. "You're looking at it."

"You mean you requested this teeny box that once served as home to canned peas?" I asked, realizing we had a recurring theme here. Then, I asked her to help me understand why cats treated boxes as if they were upholstered in mackerel.

She scowled. "Tell me why you idolize your room," she shot back.

Oh brother, what a sharp-tongued little squirt. "Well, it's cozy, and I can practice my Spanish privately without disturbing the neighbors," I offered. "I also can hum Tony Bennett Christmas tunes in my room if I want, and I don't have to clean up or wear party clothes. And I can burp in my room, and nobody complains."

"So," said Snuggles, "can't you see that this box is *my* room? Hanging out here just makes my day run more smoothly. It's the place where I feel like my most essential me. No mice to catch. No dogs that require whacking. No *Monday Night Football* or bad news about homeless cats headlining Animal Planet TV. This humble box serves as my official Evergreen address."

I couldn't say that I understood cats any better, thanks to that little speech, but she did make a good point. It was fabulous to feel at home in your own room or whatever special place felt like your room. Snuggles caught me off guard with her question about my room, but then I thought about what made it so delightful.

First, it was just the right size for a guy of my build. I

appreciated that the landlord furnished two water buckets, so I could wash my hay in one and wet my whistle in the other. Every day I took delivery of some comfy shavings that invite napping. Andres did a fine job, helping me keep things neat. It just felt like I belonged here. Or maybe this place belonged to me or to all of us. For that matter, Madam belonged to me, and I hoped she'd say the same about me. I liked that. I liked fitting in this space. It was as if I was the last piece of a jigsaw puzzle. Me oh my, such a grand feeling. And another thing, I really liked that nearly all my neighbors were up for a game of cribbage almost any time of the day or night. These little details might sound rather dull to a cat, but they worked for me.

As for Snuggles and the Fluff Muffin, they might not play gin rummy but they felt the same about their boxes. I wondered if Evergreen's companion goat Bella thought about her room or if she just chewed any old boot that fell into it. On the other hand, Melanie and Olivia acted rather snarky about their rooms. Maybe they liked their personal space a bit too much and felt they had to protect it. It also was possible they played Scrabble together without interruptions from the rest of us. In that case, they probably felt the same about their rooms as we did. I'd have to make a note to interview them about this topic the next time we chatted.

Once I get better on the keyboard, I thought, *maybe Madam will let me bring a laptop to my room.* Then I could write more about these mysteries of life right when they arose, rather than after the fact.

28

New Year's Resolutions

It began shortly after the Christmas holiday, when the
landlord suggested I looked and smelled gamey. (Mind you, I was not
alone in this situation. Gabe and Omar weren't any too fresh either,
which made our card games a tad foul. Any event that was confined
to close quarters posed a challenge to the nose.) She meant I needed a
bath, as did my winter blanket. A haircut might also be in order,
though I wouldn't let anyone touch my mane or tail. In any case,
bathing and grooming in January didn't hold much appeal.

"And then we have the issue of your room," the landlord

added with a grimace. "This, too, could use a bit of airing out or perhaps a deep cleaning. I have a cabinet full of excellent cleaning products if you care to help," she suggested.

There she went again with that deep-cleaning nonsense. I always was suspicious of that term. It sounded like something an orthodontist might do against your will. Besides, what was the point in freshening one's room before freshening one's self? And just how did a four-legged guy freshen his room anyway? Still, my domicile had hosted many a card game and pizza party over these long winter nights. Maybe it was time to trot over to John's Hardware and purchase a load of those Glade scented oil plug-ins.

Furthermore, Madam told me that my room came with full housekeeping services, not lectures on sanitation. The recurrent showering theme made sense on the Fourth of July, following a hot workout, but not mid-winter in Minnesota. One glance out my frost-covered window said there must be better things to do with our time than dust for cobwebs. After all, my friends and I had rules about this. Once winter officially arrived, we just bundled up in our Rambo blankets and checked out of any personal housekeeping responsibilities until May.

Apparently, our rule didn't apply. Madam again appeared at the door with a bag full of my favorite, all-natural, super-silk hair care products. These, of course, were the ones I shared with special friends, including Ghillie. Not many horses would get attached to hair care items, but my attachment actually was about protecting my best assets. Remember, that fabulous mane and tail of mine made great conversation starters with those of the female persuasion. Of course, Madam knew about this little quirk of mine. When she asked me what I thought about a New Year's resolution concerning personal hygiene, I knew she planned to bribe me with hair care luxuries. I agreed to part of the bargain but put my hoof down when it came to a full body bath. We settled on a light vacuuming, with mane and tail salon services.

What I didn't understand was how all this cleanliness somehow got attached to the idea of New Year's resolutions. I wondered who made this connection, and who said we really needed New Year's resolutions anyway. Maybe these doomed promises were designed to make us feel guilty about our personal appearance or lack of exercise? It was about time to conduct a bit of research.

The next morning at breakfast, I asked Omar and Bingo what they planned to do about New Year's resolutions. Omar stopped chewing long enough to look perplexed. Resolutions of any type didn't interest him much, especially when they involved work, speed, or dieting.

"If you don't mind, I think I'll just resolve to join you on tour in the Comfy Sundowner," he replied. "You should have your book done soon, so we can just ride around all year, promoting it." He then turned a loving gaze back to his feed bucket. This seemed like a fitting resolution for Omar; plus, I looked forward to the company of a travel companion.

Bingo, on the other hand, announced he planned to take up "eventing." This particular discipline involved a cross-country sprint over tall jumps and water hazards, plus a bit of dressage to top it off. Eventing, from my perspective, required speed, agility, and a heart the size of a soccer ball. Bingo enjoys many worthy talents, but this did not sound like one of them. It reminded me of Madam's wish to drive an Indy 500 pace car. For that matter, speed and athleticism didn't come to mind with either Omar or Bingo. Shuffleboard, with heavy hors d'oeuvres, would be more fitting. Nonetheless, I listened and took notes as Bingo regaled us with all the ways he planned to extinguish his competition. It was a little frightening to hear, coming from the mouth of such a shy guy. Thankfully, he couldn't leap into this new sport until spring, which gave us a few months to talk him out of it.

"And just what kind of resolution do you have in mind?" Omar queried. "Entering one of your carrot cakes in the Pillsbury Bake-Off?" He snickered.

"Well, that's a fantastic idea," I agreed, "but I've been thinking more along the lines of a genealogy project." After all, Evergreen recently entered the wireless age. All I had to do was slip into our office, boot up the computer, and jump on to Ancestry.com."

"Why?" asked Omar. He could tell my resolution involved more work than he thought necessary. Certainly, it looked like more work than touring in the Comfy Sundowner. "Are you worried you might find an uncle who robbed banks?" he chuckled.

"You never know. I might find out that Seabiscuit was my second cousin," I offered. "Or perhaps my next of kin includes the world champion cutting horse, Mr. San Peppy. Priceless nuggets of family history might come to light. In any case, learning more about who I am could explain why I keep testing all these new careers."

"True," agreed Omar.

These guys didn't sound very convincing with their New Year's resolution ideas, so I tried to interview a couple more Evergreen residents, Gabe and Olivia. That went absolutely nowhere. Next, I spoke with Prince, the petulant pony. He just scowled at the mention of resolutions.

Undeterred by everyone's lack of interest, I decided to try a different tack, one with which they could identify—weight management. All those holiday cookies had taken a toll on our physiques. Even Patrick's partner, Kay, was asking Madam if she could borrow her largest girth, due to Patrick's expanded mid-section. Frankly, most members of Evergreen's herd looked a smidge soft around the edges. Maybe this was what they meant when they talked about muffin tops. That was because our favorite winter recreation leaned toward tea and cookies, rather than core crunching or spinning classes. Horseopoly also provided hours of relaxing activity, as did John Wayne movies. We happened to prefer quiet pastimes to get us through the long winter evenings. Here was my opportunity to fire up the troops with exercise. If we didn't do something, we'd all be ordering new wardrobes by May.

Therefore, I immediately began investigating body-sculpting solutions. These were all the rage. I scoured the Cutting Horse Chatter and the Washington County Extension catalog. Even the Chronicle of the Horse lists a few ideas about winter diet and exercise. Every day, a pile of brochures arrived in my mailbox. Amazingly, the brochures actually sparked some interest, even among our most committed couch potatoes. Maybe it was the pictures that grabbed their attention. One featured a group of strapping geldings decked out in horse aerobics outfits. Another, the Slim Down Sous Chef cooking class, spotlighted an obese Clydesdale wearing a chef's hat. Then we had the before-and-after photo of a dressage horse, gracing the cover of Pilates by Paula. Last of all, Yolanda's Yoga Emporium's featured a curious snapshot of one of Yolanda's students asleep in a yoga pose. I couldn't imagine any of the Evergreen guys going for a pair of Spandex tights, but they certainly acted interested.

Now that I had everyone's attention, I pondered which class we should go for. My answer arrived when Olivia dropped in with her hat-snacking companion. She plucked my exercise class list from me, surveyed the selection, and handed it back with a dramatic sigh.

"How about ballroom dance," she suggested with a wink. Olivia might be a scary girl, but she did come up with some sterling ideas. Aretha Thoroughbred Dance Studio would arrive next Tuesday morning at 10:00.

29

Beating the Winter Blahs

They say Minnesota authors get more work done because winter months keep them indoors and kindle their creative juices. Or was it their productive juices? In our case, it might be their snacking and relaxation juices. Any one of these seemed to fit hand-in-hand with winter in the northern part of the country. I tried to exercise a bit of self-discipline with my blogging and posting on my Facebook fan page, but it wasn't easy.

Madam thought we should take advantage of the less active season by signing up for a writing conference. I agreed, and so we took part in an Erma Bombeck Humor Writer's Conference. Not only did I work on my humor-writing skills, but I even joined a humor writer's chat group. This came as quite a surprise to the group members, as nobody had ever met a horse humorist. Apparently, they needed some convincing, so they asked me to blog about my Erma experience before making me an official member. I also offered sensitivity training for chat group members on what makes a politically incorrect horse joke.

Beyond the Erma conference, winter at Evergreen Farm settled into a quiet pattern—make that boring. Blah. Dull, In need of sparkling entertainment ideas. According to Omar, a few sparkling ideas started making the rounds. He claimed the catalyst for this was climate change. He said winter used to be *real* winter here in the north. Everybody's garden hose froze solid by Thanksgiving. Then, a couple feet of snow fell, bringing out the shovels and fortifying the chiropractic business. After that, everyone groused about the weather until spring. This winter, however, couldn't seem to get started, though I heard local meteorologists proclaiming that a "Snowmageddon" event was coming our way.

As a native Oklahoman, I did know something about weather. The last time Madam and I visited friends in that state, we witnessed several bracing seasons in one afternoon. The first day we nearly fainted, rounding up yearling colts in 106-degree heat. It was so parched, even the water moccasins couldn't muster energy to strike. Twelve hours later, the temperature dropped sixty degrees. This kind of change, accompanied by a torrent of rain and wind, causes Oklahomans to simply shrug. Minnesotans, on the other hand, start e-mailing relatives from Ohio to Stockholm reporting every detail about winter weather. It must be a Scandinavian thing.

I started to see a pattern. First, the radio would predict an incoming storm lurking in the Rocky Mountains. Next, two-thirds of Twin Cities' residents would jump in their SUVs and head for the grocery store. Convinced the weather warnings meant an onslaught of homebound husbands and children, women would pull out board games and jigsaw puzzles. Mothers queued up movies on their Apple TVs. Even the Evergreen landlords drove posthaste to the Maple Plain Co-op to top up our grain supply.

Back to Omar's report that sparkling entertainment ideas have been floating about: he said that some of the new winter activity trends included cattle and others involved guns. And he wasn't talking about dairy cattle or about Lyle Anderson's Angus herd down the road. Nor was he referring to some innocent trapshooting event at the Long Lake Field and Gun Club. He told me stories about team penning and mounted cowboy shooting. What really was strange was that these stories were coming from the mouths of local dressage horses, not cow ponies.

Let me explain. Team penning might look like fun to the average spectator, but it involves maneuvers best suited to those who understand the ways of cattle. This is a timed event that requires speedy sorting and moving cows from one point to another. As for mounted cowboy shooting, this too is no leisurely game of golf. It demands both speed and calm in the midst of gunfire. Granted, the guns shoot blanks, but there's nothing fake about the fire. Competitors dress in period cowboy outfits and blaze away at balloons mounted to posts. The trick is to gallop at top speed, break all the balloons, and avoid landing in the dirt or making an unscheduled exit from the arena. Neither the costumes nor the ground rules look anything like a dressage test. Yet according to Omar, on about January 15, dressage aficionados from all over the area started signing up for these two sports. This struck me as a tad dangerous.

Team penning and mounted cowboy shooting made sense in Arizona or New Mexico but not so much up here in cold country. We didn't see many cattle standing around in the snow, waiting to get penned. Most of our cattle spent the day waiting to get milked. Most horses didn't appreciate shots firing overhead either. Yet these ranch-style pursuits included tall warmblood horses decked out in English tack. It sounded a little embarrassing. On the other hand, fun was fun, and one must give credit to those who figured out how to beat the winter blahs. If everyone was so darn bored, though, maybe we could come up with something completely new.

When the landlord left me a note suggesting it was time to begin planning for Evergreen Farm's First Annual Winter Games, I perked right up. Even the oldsters and couch potatoes brightened at the suggestion of new games. Surely we could come up with something more fun and less likely to prompt an OSHA safety inspection. Why, just yesterday Gilbert reported that Spruce and several other senior members of our herd had taken up match racing in the pasture. Talk about a broken bone looking for a place to happen. Maybe we could get them to sign up for ping-pong in the barn aisle.

I jumped into action. For starters, I appointed committee chairs, and everyone accepted—and more volunteers kept showing up at the door. Ms. Fendi and Ms. Melanie agreed to take charge of the square dance competition, including music selections. A few eager retirees from Fortuna Farm signed up for this event. Ms. Fendi reminded me the she knew her way around the kitchen, so I invited her to create a menu for the potluck picnic.

Olivia insisted she could do justice to the decorations and serve the food, though I wasn't sure her companion Bella made the best assistant. Bella ate anything, from discarded overshoes to wet tennis balls and, of course, my hats! I hoped this wouldn't interfere with the food service.

Good old Gabe volunteered to run the cribbage tournament. I thought Gabe spent a little too much time studying online cribbage techniques, including cribbage CliffsNotes. He rarely lost a game, a detail that caused some to wonder if he had discovered more than CliffsNotes. As long as he played by the rules, though, he should be able to manage a tournament.

The pony board game committee—Prince, Gilbert, NoDak, and Buddy—insisted we offer Trivial Pony Pursuit. These undersized chaps liked to show off their smarts. They made first-rate Words with Friends players too, and they had lots of friends willing to sign up to play. NoDak had earned a reputation for winning at five-card draw. These were the kind of talents that sprang from long winter evenings with nothing else to do but practice card games.

Everyone had a job, leaving me to put together the hoofleball play-offs. This spirited competition looked like broomball without brooms. It required teams of six, plus a goalie and a team captain. I faced some challenges, due to age and talent. We were a bit long on age and short on talent, and the roster included a diverse group in both categories. As much as we all loved diversity, we were missing some key positions.

Omar fell into the slow-but-sure category. Spruce couldn't remember if we played with a ball or a puck. Skip the Champagne ran with such passion that he kept jumping over the goal, rather than whacking the ball into it. Fortunately, we did have Clyde for a goalie. He was stout enough to block goals, yet nimble enough to supervise safety. We needed both.

Once our First Annual Evergreen Winter Games were officially in production, it was time to start thinking about a guest list. Maybe those big warmbloods who thought they could pen cattle would consider joining us, thus giving the cows a break. They might even like to play a hand or two of Texas Hold'em, or maybe a two-step around the barn with Olivia would bring them to their senses. That might even bring Olivia to her senses. I intended to bring my laptop and camera to record this premier event.

Maybe winter really did spark our creative juices. Our little herd of climate-challenged equines came up with a grand winter party plan.

30

A Texas Tale

It happened again. Information sailing around Evergreen suggested that Madam had omitted some important details from our daily chin-wags. This rumor came to my attention when I overheard the landlord talking about another new horse planning to move in. Not just *any* horse but another of Madam's horses. *For Pete's sake, this woman must run a horse rescue business*, I thought. *I certainly have a question or two for her.* It looked like I was about to get my opportunity to interview her when she strolled in the front door, asking if I cared to join her on a little road trip.

"Well, um, okay," I mumbled. She really caught me off guard with her surprise arrival and then a curious invitation. *This must be some kind of scheme*, I thought, *as she knows full well how long the winter has been and how much I love road trips.* "But first, how about sharing a little background material on this *other* horse of yours," I suggested. "A second horse, I might add."

"Ah, yes, I was wondering when you would ask about that," she replied breezily, as if unveiling a new horse every few weeks was a common occurrence. "You see, Noah, I actually have three horses— Ghillie, whom you know, and Thistle, whom you are about to meet. But first, we must rescue her and bring her home in your Comfy Sundowner trailer."

That's it! She is running a rescue operation! "Who, may I ask, is Thistle, and why does this individual require rescuing?" I queried as calmly as possible. "Has she been taken hostage by foreign nationals? Is she living with a bunch of hippies?"

"No, she's a young mare I sent to Texas to sell," Madam patiently explained. "She's a talented cow horse with a bright future, but cow horses find very few job opportunities in Minnesota. They tend to have more success in places like Texas and Oklahoma. I was told that a nice family bought her for their daughter, but I've now learned differently."

Considering the success of our First Annual Winter Games, at least we agreed that this was not great cow horse country. She then filled in more details. Thistle disappeared from a ranch in Nowthen, Texas, where she was being shown to prospective buyers. After making phone calls to friends in that area, Madam realized something was amiss. Apparently, there was no prospective buyer, but the horse had disappeared. That's when she decided to take matters into her own hands. She now planned to travel to Texas and retrieve Thistle from the hands of a probable horse thief. My assignment, should I choose to accept it, was to offer moral support to the horse-napped Thistle. Of course, that was assuming we found her.

Boy oh boy, what have I stuck my hoof into now? I wondered. *Just when I was settling in to this charmed new life, we're driving back down south, with a tricky stop in Nowthen, Texas.* Nothing good could be happening in Nowthen. It seemed like a lot of miles to travel to repossess Madam's third horse. Besides, I didn't know how Texans felt about a woman nabbing her own horse. This sounded complicated.

Nonetheless, the plan went together quickly. Madam's friend Georgine would accompany us as a spotter or maybe as a referee. This depended on whether or not we ran into a cowboy named Chip. Word had it that Chip might have spirited the horse off to a little hideaway near his place. Anyway, Georgine was a professional photographer and possessed some powerful camera lenses. According to her, these things worked like big binoculars, meaning she could spot miscellaneous stolen horses a half mile away. As the official spotter, Georgine planned to survey the territory with her oversized lens, in hopes of discovering the absent Thistle. By the way, the territory she intended to survey consisted of some thirty thousand acres—a questionable plan. Madam's expanding horse collection was starting to trouble me. Not only was I now one of three horses, but I could already see my meager book profits going into horse feed and boarding bills for the rest of our growing family.

It was with some anxiety that I stepped into the Comfy Sundowner and departed from Evergreen's welcoming driveway. Madam and Georgine didn't know how to program the GPS, so I suggested we buy a map, drive straight south on Interstate 35W, and simply look for the Nowthen exit. They both agreed.

Since the Comfy Sundowner could accommodate only two of us, I was on my own until we rounded up this Thistle horse. Even her name sounded prickly. If this indicated anything about her personality, it was no surprise Madam decided to find her a new home. Anyhoo, Madam was kind enough to rig up my radio, so Taylor Swift and Brad Paisley could keep me company on the long drive.

We stopped for a layover with Georgine's family in Topeka, the only sensible decision at that point. I bunked with a couple of hunting mules that liked to entertain one another with Ole and Lena jokes (sometimes referred to as Minnesota jokes). These two insisted they'd seen me in the movie *Fargo*. Slim chance the Cohen brothers had hired any horses for that movie, but I nodded civilly. Fortunately, these fellows played a Kansas City version of rummy, so we managed to get through the evening.

I was anxious; we'd been on the road all day, and I already missed my room. I even missed the barn cats and the landlords. For some reason, I'd rather endure a tube worming from Dr. Carlson than come face-to-face with a cowboy named Chip. Surely he was going to have a lot of questions about why we wanted to transport one of *his* horses back up north. We could only hope he didn't drive a pickup with a fully loaded gun rack.

Early the next morning, we pulled out again. I cranked my country music up high, and lead-foot Madam pushed the Ram pickup past 70 mph. At this point, I kept thinking that a slow drive up the Gunflint Trail seemed much safer and more rewarding than a speeding pickup truck ride south on an interstate. Meanwhile, Georgine had assembled her camera and was surveying the landscape, making adjustments by focusing on road kill. It struck me as magical thinking that she could use a camera to pick out a single horse on thirty thousand acres. And we were operating strictly on hearsay. This whole plot grew out of two phone calls to horsemen, who recommended that Madam come immediately to collect her mare. Incidentally, neither guy volunteered to help with this caper. So armed only with a set of AQHA papers and a pal with an oversized camera lens, she proposed to round up her lost cow horse. It was enough to bring on a migraine headache.

We passed a sign that read "Nowthen, exit 29, one-half mile," and Madam took the exit rather speedily, heading west to nowhere. Or maybe we were heading for a Texas jail. The next ten miles were uneventful, except for a few potholes and an armadillo sunbathing in the road. Some surprised cows looked up as we passed, but there was no sign of Ms. Cow Horse. Finally, Madam pulled up on the side of the road. It looked like she and Georgine were making adjustments to their plan. They jumped back in the pickup, Madam tromped on the gas, and off we went again. She then turned south in a cloud of yellow dust and drove too fast for conditions. After another five or six miles, Georgine suddenly yelled, "Stop!"

"Why?" Madam shouted back, so startled she nearly hit the ditch, with me in the Comfy Sundowner. Instead, she hit the brakes, causing my radio to take flight out of the hay net where it'd been anchored for the past six hours. My windows didn't give me a full view, but I could see Georgine jump out of the truck and take a gander across the field through her ten-pound camera lens.

"I think I might have found her!" she proclaimed triumphantly.

Madam jammed the truck into park and stumbled out on to the

road to have a look. At this point, neither woman even remembered she'd brought me along. To be fair, they only brought me as a member of the horse-napping team, but I was nothing more than a prisoner in my own trailer.

After passing the camera back and forth several times, Madam and Georgine agreed that it looked like Thistle. Through no solid plan of their own, they actually found the lost mare—and in good old Chip's pasture, no less. *So now what do we do?* I wondered, though couldn't ask, due to my prisoner status. The answer came quickly anyway.

"Get in," barked Madam. "I've got the registration papers. We're going to the Nowthen Sheriff's Department to request a little assistance. I'm sure when I show the sheriff these documents, she will come right on out here and help us load up this mare."

These two were starting to remind me of *Thelma and Louise*! Thank heaven neither of them decided to bring firearms. (Or had they? Oh dear.)

I was having bad feelings about the operation in which I now was stuck. The Nowthen sheriff might or might not find Madam's horse-napping strategy an excellent plan. The sheriff might also be downtown enjoying a fried pie and a cup of coffee or attending a city council meeting. For all we knew, the sheriff moonlighted for Cowboy Chip. I thought these all were good possibilities, not that anybody intended to consult me about such matters. I really needed to start cultivating a stronger voice when it came to family decision making.

Once more, Madam burned gravel with the big Ram truck. Was it possible she'd forgotten she was hauling a trailer with her favorite horse inside? Maybe. It was another white-knuckle ride to Nowthen, about five miles from the scene of the pending transaction. By now, my radio had covered every square inch of the Comfy Sundowner, banging my ankles as we made the corners. It was emitting only white noise at this point. We made it to town in a flash, and Madam squawked to a stop in front of the Nowthen Police Department. *I'm making a note that she must sign up for one of those senior drivers classes*, I thought, *if and when we ever get home*. Fortunately, it was Texas, and nobody paid any attention to the truck and trailer parked at an angle directly in front of the "offenders" entrance to the county jail.

Both Madam and Georgine hopped out and locked the truck, like a couple of Twin Cities girls on their way to the Southdale Mall. Heads held high, they exuded an air of confidence as they strode toward the building. Madam pulled Thistle's registration papers from her bag. I was starting to hyperventilate, just watching them, but of course, I could do nothing because I still was a prisoner in my own trailer. Ten minutes passed. I kept reminding myself that the sheriff was probably having a ham sandwich with friends somewhere. Then twenty minutes went by. Then, a half hour passed. No sign of the women wearing gracious smiles for all the help they were getting from Sheriff Bob. Then, the offender door burst open, and out they came, with Madam in the lead at a dead run. No sign of a sheriff.

We now were headed down the main street of Nowthen. I thought she was aiming north, back in the direction from which we arrived, but I still had this sinking feeling. That feeling was confirmed later when I learned just how unimpressed the sheriff was with the Georgine and Madam's horse-napping plan. Apparently, he took one squint at Thistle's registration papers and proclaimed that his cousin Jerome could produce a set of papers just as good as those. According to Georgine, the meeting came to an end after Sheriff Bob called Madam "sugar" for a third time. He then suggested she might want to track down a court order that would enable her to take her horse home. The necessary judge, according to Sheriff Bob, was currently on an Alaskan cruise with his in-laws and would not be returning to court until next Monday.

We made it back to Cowboy Chip's country estate in record time. Georgine was out on the road before the Ram came to a complete stop. Madam sprinted around the Comfy Sundowner, yanked open the tailgate, and grabbed a halter and rope. She started to run. Madam doesn't usually run. The mare was hanging out with a few others horses about a city block away. She showed no sign of helping the cause. This was not new, according to Georgine who continued to snap pictures as evidence. Madam continued to run, while all the horses except Thistle took off as if they'd just witnessed a barn fire. Thistle just stood and stared at Madam, who now was bearing down on her.

By the time Madam reached Thistle, she was out of wind but managed to get the halter on the mare. Then, she made a giant leap—another unusual move for Madam—and somehow made it onto Thistle's back and walloped her with the rope. Now they both were bearing down on us at a full gallop. Georgine ran to open the gate, and Madam and Thistle charged through. They never even stopped at the trailer ramp but ducked their heads and sailed right on in. With that, Madam slipped off, tied Thistle, tossed in a flake of hay, and locked up the tailgate—it was an impressive performance from a woman who requires a mounting block to climb on a bicycle. The meeting in Sheriff Bob's office must have been inspiring!

Thistle and I exchange quick how-dos, and down the road we went again, this time pointing north toward Oklahoma City. Madam told me later about their law enforcement meeting in Nowthen. It seemed the sheriff felt duty bound to notify Cowboy Chip of our arrival. One thing led to another, and Madam and Georgine exchanged looks with one another, confirming it was time to leave. That's when they burst out the door. That also explained a white pickup and stock trailer heading our way as we left the horse-napping scene— Cowboy Chip, no doubt! This also explained why Madam stood on the accelerator until we exited the state of Texas. It was probably the best idea she'd had all day.

Once we made it to Oklahoma, everyone calmed down. We nipped into an all-night rest stop to relax and review our travel itinerary. Madam decided to deliver Thistle to Jasper Wright's place instead of bringing her back to Evergreen. The mare had begun her career with Jasper, and the two of them seem blessed with similar dispositions. Besides, Jasper claimed he knew a family with two teenage girls who were looking for a good team penning horse. That sounded like a perfect place for Thistle and equally agreeable to me. Frankly, I wasn't disappointed to drop her off at Jasper's place. With all Madam's secret horses showing up, we needed to leave room for any additional surprises.

After many hours on the road, we finally arrived at Jasper's, late the next evening. Exhausted by their horse-napping, Madam opened the tailgate and let Thistle back out on her own. We all just stood and stared at her in disbelief. Hard to know how Georgine's camera led to all this. Harder still to believe Thistle had agreed to be caught, ridden, and loaded. And as an extra bonus, she didn't kick the tailgate off the trailer on the return home. Nobody even mentioned her adverse trailer behavior until we got to Des Moines.

As the man known for his tradition of silence, Jasper just looked us over and took a wordless walk around Thistle. Then he looked at the women again. He seemed to be having trouble digesting the fact they'd driven to Nowthen, Texas, and repossessed Madam's horse. We all stood for an awkward minute, waiting to hear what he had to say.

"Well … it looks like you girls brought home the right horse anyhow," he finally muttered. Then he led Thistle to the barn without further comment.

31

A Valentine Shortage

It was nearly Valentine's Day, and I seemed to have come up short in the sweetheart department. Not because I didn't work at it. Goodness, my skills and interests were expanding by the day. Take my Spanish lessons. I'd been at that since meeting a lovely Andalusian mare in Baker Park. Unfortunately, Evergreen's residents consisted primarily of German females, which didn't give me many opportunities to speak Spanish, but that was beside the point. At least I practiced with Jesus and Andres, so I'd be ready for the day any Spanish-speaking beauties came my way.

And how about my rock-star hair? All the silk hair products I purchased online really did add dazzle to my fashionably long locks. If that wasn't enough, I continued taking baking classes with the King Charles Flour whiz-bang pastry chef. I could turn out a luscious gingerbread and a batch of bran muffins that would make most girls weep. But instead of weeping, they'd blink sweetly and ask me to introduce them to one of my friends. Or sometimes they'd just ask me for directions to the park. Even Madam's mare Thistle didn't exactly warm up to me after our bold rescue operation and that long ride back from Texas. What the heck was wrong that I had so much trouble finding a girlfriend?

Take the subject of civil discourse. Typically, this appealed to females, but Mrs. Landlord continued to remind me that I talked too much. What she didn't know was I could chat intelligently about many things, including Ireland or Montana or even the Minnesota state fair's Oink Booth. And how many guys can sit down and play a lively game of hearts with a girl? Not many! I guess even a good résumé and lots of assets don't always help a guy land a valentine.

Of course, Madam said I was constantly falling for the wrong kind of girls. "Why don't you choose someone who doesn't just gaze at herself in the dressage mirrors?" she suggested. "And surely you must know that pinned ears are not a sign of affection or a potential friendship," she added. "Noah, you just need to pick a girl who better suits your personality."

For heaven's sake, they *all* didn't behave rudely. Even Faith sometimes spoke nicely to me. And Ms. Fendi did agree to have tea and cake that one time. Even the neighbor girl who was sending mean e-mails to Omar turned out to be okay. Maybe it was the warmblood females who didn't find appendix quarter horses very interesting. That was all the more reason to keep working on my cow horse skills. It was just possible I belonged out there on the range, hanging with a bunch of Herefords.

Anyhoo, Omar and I were discussing our courting quandary over a piece of the aforementioned gingerbread and a cup of tea. He got me started on tea because none of us could work Evergreen's coffeemaker. Besides, since my Irish travels, I preferred tea to the lukewarm decaf they served in this establishment. Come to think of it, a tea-drinking fellow should also appeal to girls, though that didn't seem to be the case with some of us. Maybe I was just trying too hard.

All this caused me to review my valentine prospects from recent months. Maybe I could learn something from my mistakes. Let me share my experience with Faith, as an example. Ah, what a beauty she was! I say "was," because she left Evergreen for greener pastures. Anyway, this lovely creature captured my heart the day we met. Madam was correct, though; Faith presented a formidable challenge. She played hard to get, though most would call that an understatement. I showered Faith with carrots and best intentions, but nothing worked. I even gave her my radio and convinced her to take a garden tour around Lake Minnetonka in the Comfy Sundowner. No matter. For all my ardor and hard work, she ran off with a flashy Lusitano stud. They now are expecting their first baby and live in New Mexico.

Next came Olivia. She presented three or four challenges. First, everyone knew Olivia traveled with her companion, Bella. I happen to collect fine hats, and Bella ate two of my favorite hats before we even had a chance to get acquainted. Second, Olivia did not apologize for the hat-eating episode. In fact, she must have missed all the classes on manners, including ground manners or any other kind of etiquette. She could flatten anything from a barn cat to a stable hand with no warning. She also felt the need to protect Bella by flashing a fine set of teeth in the process. Even Wally stayed in the house when Olivia made her entrance in her paddock. It was not uncommon to see Andres dive for cover when asking her to come in from the pasture. Even Bella spent a good bit of time running for her life when in the company of Olivia.

Madam often said that Olivia could convince a horse lover to buy a llama instead of a horse. But I have to admit Olivia was a looker! Our entire cribbage club suffered from weak knees whenever she strutted past the game room. They all fell for her, but nobody mustered the courage to ask her out. Well, I sort of did. It was a pretty lame attempt, and it did not go particularly well.

Then came our two newest feminine members of the Evergreen family—Ms. Fendi and Melanie. I enjoyed some initial success wooing them with my new culinary skills, but in the end, they remained standoffish. That could be the warmblood thing Madam mentioned. Maybe warmbloods and quarter horses truly don't mix well, though I can't think of any good reason why they wouldn't. Anyway, even Gabe said that most the girls I picked reminded him of his cousin Muriel, a law enforcement officer for a sheep ranch in Arizona. However, I think appointing Ms. Fendi and Melanie co-chairs of our Evergreen Winter Games Square Dance Contest was a good move. Some two-stepping with the neighbors really loosened them up.

Omar seemed to do a little better than I did in the girl department. Not that he had a steady girlfriend, but at least Gracie chatted him up with local gossip. And then there was the Powder Puff stalker from down the road, the one who finally apologized for hurting his feelings and eventually playing a few rounds of cards with us. She might not have qualified as a date but at least she provided a brief tête-à-tête with Omar that made him feel better about himself.

All this reminiscing led to today. Here we were, Omar and I, feeling a little blue about our empty dance cards on Valentine's Day. So I asked him to tell me what he thought it meant to be a valentine.

"Er, it's about girls, isn't it?" he asked hesitantly "We don't have girlfriends. We don't even have girls who are friends," he added glumly.

I offered to give it a try. "You know everybody thinks Valentine's Day is only about girls and flowers and romance," I began. "But Madam sends frilly cards to her friends and to her kids, even though they all have outgrown frilly valentines."

"That's nice," said Omar.

"Even the landlords made reservations at McCafferty's Pub tonight for a valentine dinner," I added. "And Andres and his wife plan to step out to a dance club. Isn't that all about being friends? Don't you think a valentine can mean more than romance? How about a fun chum or a fine friend? Or why not make it a pleasing pal? Or even a charming cribbage cohort? You know, Omar, I'm beginning to think this romance stuff is way overrated."

"You could be right," he agreed.

All those examples I mentioned pretty much describe Omar.

He might not dance so well, and he certainly can't cook, but he's kind, and he rarely fusses or criticizes anyone in our card club The two of us might not have dates, but we could surely celebrate Valentine's Day with a good John Wayne movie and a cold Bud!

32

Speaking of Success

Madam looked sad this morning. She breezed past my room and out the back door without so much as a howdy. I could tell something was out of order; I saw her sitting behind the barn with Snuggles the cat on her lap for a very long time. It was too cold outside for any serious sitting, but she showed no sign of coming in. Last night's spring snowfall covered everything but the half-frozen pond, where a few Canada geese were practicing their touchdowns. They were too early. I was still wearing my cozy winter blanket and liking to wake up in my toasty room. Madam definitely needed a hat and a better pair of mittens if she was going to hang around out there much longer. I worried because she just stared over the lower pasture. Like the geese, maybe she was looking for spring.

I was afraid, though, that it was about Ghillie. Madam has never acted like this. She always visited me first thing in the morning. Plus, a couple of us heard some hushed talk coming from Wally's Woodworking shop last night. The landlords kept saying Ghillie's name, but that's all I could make out. I needed to find out what was going on. I hoped that nobody would notice if I let myself out of my room and went to check on her. At least I could take her one of my clean blankets.

Lifting the latch on an Evergreen door was no small trick, though I was getting better at it. It was a delicate operation that required teasing it open with my teeth. As chilly as it was this morning, it was a good thing my tongue didn't freeze to the latch.

Once I was out, I saw her coming my way, with Snuggles tucked under her arm. I hoped she wouldn't mind that I'd given the landlords the slip, but there was no time to worry about that— suddenly, Madam stood directly in front of me. She just looked at me without even asking how I'd escaped. Then she looked out over the pond at the geese again. Finally, she whispered that Ghillie had died last night.

"What? How?" I demanded. "Why? Why would he die when he was getting better? Didn't you say he was getting better? Didn't he just go away to rest and get stronger? He looked great when the university made that video. He told me he just wanted to take a little break, a short vacation in Wisconsin to give him a chance to build up his strength. What happened?"

"I'm so sorry, Noah. He just never got well," Madam replied, obviously crushed by the news. "Every week became more painful for him. My friend Jane gave him the best possible care, and even his pasture pals tried to help. But in the end, he could hardly walk. The Lyme disease caused him such crippling arthritis that he could barely hobble out of his stall."

"I can't believe it. You never told me he might die."

"I didn't know he might die. It's been a year since he came

home from the university. Anyway, after several weeks of trying to keep him comfortable, Jane called me. We finally decided we had little choice, except to call the veterinarian. It was the only answer, Noah, to relieve Ghillie from his pain and end his life humanely."

"No! You can't. He's my friend," I protested. "How could this happen when he seemed to be on the mend? It's not fair."

"You're right, Noah, it isn't fair. We all had big dreams for Ghillie. His amazing talent could have taken him to the highest levels of performance and success. Sometimes there just aren't very good answers to painful questions like this one."

"Did I do something wrong?" I asked. "Was there something we should have done for him and didn't? I knew it! I never should have opened his gate and taken him for long walks around the farm. He was exhausted when we got back. Even Mr. Landlord scolded me for that." "No, no," insisted Madam. "You've done nothing to cause this. You were a good friend to Ghillie. But these past weeks I've been thinking about some things. At first, the whole situation seemed like such a failure. You know, people have asked me why I persisted with Ghillie. Wouldn't it have been much easier to put him down and be done with it? We certainly considered that route on more than one occasion. I've been asking myself some questions about this term 'success' that keeps coming up. What does it really mean? We always talk about success like it can only mean a perfect outcome and a complete victory."

"Well, of course," I agreed. "How can you argue with that?"

"Triumph. Achievement. Glory. These aren't words we connect with average or normal or even typical, do we?" she asked as she watched the geese skidding across the half-thawed pond.

"No, not really. But what does that have to do with Ghillie?"

"Our world really doesn't have much time for average," Madam continued.

Oh boy, maybe she just needs to get a few things off her chest, I thought. Meanwhile, I was feeling sick to my stomach, and my head was spinning.

"To be average is to fall short," Madam declared to the cat that contentedly kneaded her jacket. "If you believe the messages we hear today, average means not doing enough. It rates right down there with failure, a complete flop. Most of us learn that success comes only by way of achieving above-average feats. You know, like dancing and singing, or in your case, like winning horse races or performing high level dressage."

"Wait a minute," I croaked. "The governor has not exactly proclaimed National Noah's Day due to my success in either of those careers. I've probably enjoyed more success as Evergreen's entertainment director. Well, I also can sing a Spanish song that Andres taught me. But that hardly qualifies as a successful singing career."

"That's my point," said Madam, as she read the frown on my face. "Think of all we miss if we believe success only happens when we do big things? Aren't we just as successful if we do small things well?"

"Now that seems a little radical," I muttered.

Her words caused me to shiver. It was true I'd been working ever so hard to succeed—learned how to read and cook and trail cattle, not to mention memorizing reining patterns. I'd even mastered pulling a sleigh. My achievements looked pretty impressive, until this conversation got started. The whole idea about average equaling success didn't make much sense. Yet she sounded sincere, like she was not trying to fool with me. And I had to admit, for all my newly acquired skills, I didn't exactly feel successful. I decided to give her a few more minutes to make her case. Besides, I felt too awful to argue with her.

Madam continued to deliver her one-woman debate about the merits of average. Obviously, she'd been giving this a lot of thought.

"The problem with all this overachieving," she said, while carefully watching my expression, "is most of us fit nicely into the pretty average category."

Holy cow, that's a new one! I thought. *I can't say I ever thought of myself as average! Or ever wanted to think of myself as average.*

"Noah, don't we spend most of our time living common days made up of little things and ordinary dealings with one another?" she asked. "My year with Ghillie amounted to nothing more than washing and wrapping his legs and giving him his medicine. When we finished with that, I'd feed him and take him for a walk. This went on day after day for months. It was always the same simple stuff, plain little tasks that pointed him toward healing. It was a pretty routine set of interactions that made up our friendship. Every tiny improvement, every early morning greeting, and every time Ghillie indicated yes, he wanted to continue, it felt like success to me!"

Ghillie also struck me as a success, but that probably was because he treated me as if I mattered. And I suppose we never did anything too big together. But he wasn't well enough to do much either. We talked a lot, and he liked watching our hoofleball matches. He read the newspaper every day and always expressed a lot of interest in everyone else. It just felt right to be around him.

Then she took me aback by asking me to describe my idea of an average day, the kind of day I had grown into since coming to Evergreen.

"Well, um, I've never thought about anything like this. So I suppose an average day might start with a gallop down the Luce Line trail with you, of course. Maybe we could find a picnic table and have a little snack. Later, I'd go for a game of gin rummy with Patrick. Or a round of cribbage with Gabe is always fun. Then Omar and I would take a little spin in the Comfy Sundowner to Waconia Farm Supply. He likes to shop and sample the new flavored hay cubes. After that, it would be delightful to take a dive in the mud, followed by a cool bath, if I felt too sticky. Oh, and a few fresh carrots waiting in my room would be … well, it would be pretty average, since you leave carrots there all the time. Finally, after my girl troubles this past year, I'm happy to report Molly actually enjoys my company. Maybe we would take in a drive-in movie together. I guess that would pretty much cover a typical or average day, as you call it."

Madam sat and thought for a minute. "So if that's an average day, Noah, tell me what would make a great day—you know, a really successful, prize-winning day?"

I still was feeling queasy and needed to get back to my room before the landlord discovered I'd let myself out. Besides, the others didn't know yet about Ghillie, and I needed to tell them.

Madam waited for my answer.

"I'm thinking." I dilly-dallied, unsure of what she expected.

My mind was sort of blank. Then it struck me. I'd just described a great day, not an average day. "I just told you what makes a successful day," I finally replied, with mixed feelings.

"You mean an average day?" she asked.

"No. Well, I mean, yes," I murmured. "They're the same." With that, I turned and walked back to my room, sad about Ghillie and confused by Madam's questions and my answers.

The place was pretty quiet at breakfast. Mrs. Landlord had already shared the news with Evergreen's little community. Everyone, including Bella, stopped in to offer condolences. Omar brought me a bag of molasses cookies he had been saving for a special occasion. Gabe asked if I'd like to work a new jigsaw puzzle with him. Ms. Fendi offered me a cup of tea, and even Patrick asked if I would like to join him for dinner. Nothing sounded too good, but I was really glad they asked.

Late in the day, Madam came to my room and stood. "Noah, I want you to know something. Excitement, ambition, and a thousand noble causes can sometimes lift us up and bring us success. But they will never replace the reward of sharing a meal with a friend, or riding through Baker Park, or touring with you and Omar in the Comfy Sundowner," she confirmed. "It seems to me you have been enjoying that same good feeling every day you try something new or play a round of cards with your friends."

We listened to my neighbors contentedly munching their grain.

"I'm going to miss him," I finally said.

"So am I, Noah. I'm going to miss him a lot. Now, it's just the two of us, and of course the hairball pets. You do remember that you're the one who came up with that charming name, don't you?"

"Yes, but that doesn't mean I don't like them! I do like them. I like a lot of things."

"I know. That's what I like about you. You have a way of saying thank-you for what has been and yes to what's lies ahead. Many of us find it much easier to say no than yes, but you're one of those who prefers to say yes."

The two of us just hung out there for a while, keeping one another company. She sat on a mounting block with the same cat on her lap that had kept her company all morning. There really wasn't much to say, so we said nothing. About the time Andres showed up with my dinner, Madam stood up and got ready to leave.

"How would you like to come with me to the Minnesota Horse Expo this weekend?" she asked.

"Of course," I answered with unexpected gusto. "Can we bring Omar?

"Absolutely," she said. "That's my guy!"

It's a very good thing that Madam has me to look after her.

Discussion Guide

At the beginning of the book we read: "We live in difficult times with no shortage of bad news and uninvited events. Yet even difficult times cannot take away our capacity to hope—to listen, learn, laugh and be transformed."

In what ways do you think Noah listens, learns, and is transformed by his friendships and travels?

Hope is a popular word we often use when talking about specific outcomes. For example, we hope our team wins or we hope to get a new car. We hope our children stay safe, and we hope to enjoy good health.

Do hope and optimism mean the same thing?

Is Noah a hopeful character or an optimistic character? Why do you think so?

Name something you feel hopeful about.

Name something you feel optimistic about.

Chapter 4 Never Say Neigh

Noah likes the word yes. He believes that yes broadens the possibilities for friendships and fun. For him, yes feels like a pathway to new things and exciting possibilities. Too much no creates needless anxiety and missed opportunities.

How does an attitude of yes or no play out in the connection between the two girls and the cranky old horseman, Bob Stall?

What does the old man gain from that connection?

What does Madam gain?

Have you ever accidently or intentionally broken into the life of a reclusive, unsociable person? If so, what was that experience like?

 Do you think it's easier for most of us to say yes or no to new ideas and possibilities? Why?

Chapter 8 Meeting Ghillie

When Noah meets Ghillie he's taken aback when Ghillie asks him, "Are you living the life that wants to live in you?"

What do you think Ghillie means by that question?

What would you say if someone asked you the same question?

Name some blessings or obstacles that enable or prevent you from living the life that wants to live in you?

Chapter 17 No Bullying

When Noah discovers that someone is bullying Omar, one of his first remarks is, "… those hooligans know nothing about Omar except that he is big and sort of fluffy."

How does knowing someone make it easier or harder to bully or gossip about him or her?

The bully turns out to be someone other than the hooligan guys they first suspect. What, if anything, does that say about one's tendency to make quick character judgments?

Noah comes up with his own solution to the bullying problem that he later shares with Ghillie. Do you think his solution succeeds? Why or why not?

Chapter 22 The Goat Companion Question

Throughout the book, Noah keeps testing new career paths. In this chapter he dithers about this. In his words, "The State Fair offered a blizzard of new vocational ideas, as if I needed anymore confusion around that topic."

He seems to equate his vocational dilemma with an identity crisis? Do you think he ever resolves either or both of those conundrums?

What role, if any, do our interests or professions play in our identity?

Chapter 27 Kitty Mysteries

Noah interviews two cats and asks what kind of gift they want for Christmas or Hanukkah or their birthday. Both cats say they want nothing more than the cardboard boxes they sleep in and call home.

How do the cats' snoozing boxes influence their wellbeing?

Do you have a comparable space or place in your life that you treasure? How do you feel when you're in that space or place?

Chapter 32 Speaking of Success

When Madam tells Noah that his friend Ghillie has died, Noah immediately asks, "Why?"

Most of us have known someone or have had a personally painful experience that has prompted us to ask, "Why?" What other kinds of questions come to mind following a loss or life-threatening illness?

In the final chapter Madam surprises Noah with her interpretation of the word success. She also offers an uncommon description of the term average.

Did you find her interpretation of success convincing?

Why or why not?

What about her analysis of average?

Overarching Themes

What specific themes did the author emphasize throughout the book? What do you think she is trying to get across to the reader?

Can you relate to the characters' predicaments? In what way do they remind you of yourself or someone you know?

Glossary

The following glossary offers readers who are new to the world of horses and horse gear a bit of insight. I've also included a few unusual-sounding Irish and Norwegian terms that have found their way into Noah's vocabulary.

Blinkers: also known as blinders or winkers; a piece of horse tack that prevents the horse from seeing to the rear and sometimes to the side. They are usually made of leather and are attached to the bridle and placed on either side of the eyes.

Cavaletti: small jumps consisting of simple rails and used for basic horse training.

Eventing: an equestrian event in which a single horse-and-rider combination competes against other combinations across three disciplines—dressage, cross-county, and show jumping.

Flagging: a training tool consisting of a four-foot-long training stick with a plastic grocery bag attached to the end. Its purpose is to gently introduce a horse to being touched on different parts of its body, while keeping the handler out of harm's way.

Ghillie: a term used in Scotland and Ireland that typically refers to a person who acts as a fishing or hunting guide.

Hobbles: a tethering device attached to one or more legs that prevents or limits a horse from wandering off.

Mounted cowboy shooting: a competitive event that requires riders to dress in classic western costumes and shoot two single-action revolvers, each loaded with five blank cartridges. A timed event, the goal is to shoot ten targets arranged in a riding arena.

Natural horsemanship: sometimes known as horse whispering; refers to a variety of horse training methods that develop a rapport with a horse by applying communication techniques derived from observing free-roaming horses. Natural horsemanship rejects abusive training methods.

Norwegian Pols and Springleik: dances, originating in eastern Norway, that travel around the room, similar to the Swedish polska.

Overcheck: a strap that goes from the middle of a driving harness, up the horse's neck, between its ears, and down the front of the bridle. It is designed to keep a horse's head up, so it can't canter or buck.

Skijoring: a sport typically involving a dog (or horse) that assists a cross-country skier by running and pulling the skier behind the animal.

Sulky: a lightweight, two-wheeled, single-seat cart used in harness racing and as a form of rural transport in many parts of the world.

Team penning: an event that gives a team of three riders on horseback from 60 to 90 seconds to separate three specifically identified cattle from a herd of 30, and put them into a 16x24 foot pen through a 10 ten-foot opening.

Triple Oxer: an oxer is a type of horse jump consisting of two rails that can be set even or uneven. A triple oxer is similar but consists of three rails in graduating height, making it more difficult to jump.